Contents

Introduction

This book is designed to help you revise for the AQA English Language A level and works alongside the *AQA A Level English Language Student Book.* As you probably already know – because you've been studying language on this course – 'to revise' can mean 'to look at again', so this book will not go through the basics and explain them, but instead test you on what you know and help you to build on the skills, knowledge and understanding of some of the main areas of the course that you already have.

It won't tell you everything you need to know but it will help you develop what you know and give you ideas for further reflection. Along the way, it will give you short activities that feature extracts for analysis and discussion, longer texts in exam-style questions and ideas about approaching the kinds of questions that might appear in the examinations.

While there is plenty of familiar material in this book to help you with different types of examination questions and Assessment Objectives, we've tried hard to offer some new material too: not because we want to bombard you with new ideas, but because the English language is always changing and being debated and there is so much that you can bring in to help you engage with the subject.

Not everything is covered here and, as always, revision is not just about last-minute cramming, but if you use the book as the course goes on you should be able to develop your exam technique, piece together links between different areas of the course and develop a better overview of the ways in which this course approaches language study.

A

Dan Clayton
Angie Kolaric

SERIES EDITOR:
Angela Goddard

OXFORD

OXFORD
UNIVERSITY PRESS

Great Clarendon Street, Oxford, OX2 6DP, United Kingdom

Oxford University Press is a department of the University of Oxford. It furthers the University's objective of excellence in research, scholarship, and education by publishing worldwide. Oxford is a registered trade mark of Oxford University Press in the UK and in certain other countries

© Oxford University Press 2018

The moral rights of the authors have been asserted

British Library Cataloguing in Publication Data
Data available

ISBN 978-019-842-670-7

10 9 8 7 6 5 4 3 2 1

Printed in China by Leo Paper Products Ltd

We are grateful for permission to include extracts from the following copyright material:

Emma Barnett: 'Can I just say...' from 'Why you should choose your words wisely', *Good Housekeeping*, June 2016, copyright © Hearst UK 2016, used by permission of Good Housekeeping/Hearst Magazines UK.
Charlie Bayliss: extract from 'Queen's English to be WIPED OUT from London 'due to high levels of immigration'.', *Daily Express*, 29 Sept 2016, copyright © Daily Express 2016, used by permission of Daily Express/Express Syndication.
Deborah Cameron: extract from 'One word, two words, pink words, blue words', on debuk.wordpress.com, 7 Dec 2017, used by permission of the author.**Stan Carey**: extract from 'There's nowt wrong with dialects, nothing broke ass about slang', *the guardian.com*, 23 May 2016, copyright © Guardian News & Media Ltd 2016, 2018, used by permission of GNM
Rod Chester: 'Linguists launch war of words on emoji as a language debate', News.com, 21 May 2015, copyright © 2015, used under licence by permission of Copyright Agency Ltd as agent for News.com.
Dan Clayton and **Rob Drummond**: extract from *Language Diversity and World Englishes* (CUP, 2018), copyright © Cambridge University Press 2018, used by permission of the publishers.
Matthew Engel: extracts from 'Say No to the Get-Go! Americanisms swamping English so wake up and smell the coffee', *Mail on Sunday*, 29 May 2010, used by permission of the author.
Ann Friedman: extract from 'Can We Just, Like, Get Over the Way Women Talk?', *The Cut*, 9 July 2015, used by permission of New York Media.
Lane Greene: quoted in *Are Americans trashing the English language?* (Daily Watch, an Economist Films production, 2017), https://www.youtube.com/watch?v=I-WJVDDZTFY, used by permission of the author and The Economist, London.
Nick Harding: extract from 'Why are so many middle-class children Speaking in Jamaican patois?', *Daily Mail*, 11 Oct 2013, used by permission of Solo Syndication/Associated Newspapers Ltd.
Richard Herring: extract from 'Warming Up', 10 Oct 2011, on www.richardherring.com, copyright © Richard Herring 2011, used by permission of the author.**Rebecca Holman**: 'How to speak 'Menglish' - the language 'only men' understand', *Daily Telegraph*, 31 Jan 2014, copyright © Telegraph Media Group Ltd 2014, used by permission of TMG.
Stuart Jeffries: 'Black country dialect: No more waggin' for Halesowen pupils', *theguardian.com*, 17 Nov 2013, copyright © Guardian News & Media Ltd 2013, 2018, used by permission of GNM
Lindsay Johns: extract from 'Ghetto grammar robs the young of a proper voice', *London Evening Standard*, 16 Aug 2011, copyright © London Evening Standard 2011, used by permission of ESI Media.
Jonathan Jones: 'Emoji is dragging us back to the dark ages - and all we can do is smile', *theguardian.com*, 27 May 2015, copyright © Guardian News & Media Ltd 2015, 2018, used by permission of GNM
C A Lejeune: 'Horror Films: The 25 best horror films of all time', *theguardian.com*, 22 Oct 2010, Archive Film Review of Psycho, 7 Aug 1960, copyright © Guardian News & Media Ltd 2010, 2018, used by permission of GNM.
G Lemon and **R Smyth**: screengrab of cricket commentary 'Ashes 2017-2018: Australia v England third text day one-live', *theguardian.com*, 14 Dec 2017, copyright © Guardian News & Media Ltd 2017, 2018, used by permission of GNM

James McCarthy: extracts from 'Forget Butty...it's Bruv now innit! Behind the 'Jafaican' dialect on the streets of Wales', *Wales Online*, 17 Nov 2013, used by permission of Media Wales Ltd, Reach Publishing Services Ltd.
Bonnie McElhinny: extract from 'An Economy of Affect: objectivity, masculinity and the gendering of police work' in *Dislocating Masculinity: Comparative Ethnographies* edited by Andrea Cornwall and Nancy Lindisfarne (2e, Routledge, 2017), used by permission of the publishers, Taylor & Francis Group, Informa UK Ltd.
John McWhorter: extract from *Talking Back, Talking Black: Truths About America's Lingua Franca* (Bellevue Literary Press, 2017), copyright © John McWhorter 2017, used by permission of The Permissions Company, Inc. on behalf of Bellvue Literary Press, www.blpress.org.
Tracy Moore: 'Google Exec. Women, stop saying 'just' so much, you sound like children', *Jezebel*, 7 Feb 2015, copyright © Gawker Media 2015, used by permission of Wright's Media, LLC as agent for Gawker Media.
M Lynne Murphy: comment on Americanisms made on 'Americanize!: Why the Americanisation of English Is a Good Thing', BBC Radio 4, 9 Aug 2017, used by permission of M Lynne Murphy.
Robert J Podesva: table 'Frequency of falsetto occurrence across situations' in 'Phonation type as a stylistic variable: The use of falsetto in constructing a persona', *Journal of Sociolinguists* 11:4, 478 (2007), copyright © Robert J Podesva 2007, used by permission of John Wiley and Sons, Inc, via Copyright Clearance Center.
David Shariatmadari: extracts from 'So what's the problem with 'so'?', *The Guardian*, 15 Nov 2017, copyright © Guardian News & Media Ltd 2017, 2018, used by permission of GNM.
Nikesh Shukla: 'Rhyming slang is nang', *theguardian.com*, 26 Jul 2013, copyright © Guardian News & Media Ltd 2013, 2018, used by permission of GNM
Christopher Stevens: 'Don't talk garbage!... or why American words are mangling our English', *Daily Mail*, 30 May 2012, including comments that follow by James Marshall, Rochester, John, Farnborough, & Lynneguist, Brighton, used by permission of Solo Syndication/Associated Newspapers Ltd.
Matilda Stylex: 'My not fair lady' published on www.wattpad.com, used by permission of the author.
Lucy Thornton: extract from 'Aufwiedersehen to Pet..hinny..dear..darling..love..and sweetheart', *Daily Mirror*, 17 Aug 2006, used by permission of Mirrorpix, Reach Publishing Services Ltd.
Felicity Titjen: transcripts of 'Jess' with her mother first used in an AQA ENGB3 exam paper, June 2012, used by permission of Felicity Titjen.
Greg Woodin: 'accentism is a real thing - just ask us brummies', *TMRW Magazine*, 21 February 2018, used by permission of TMRW Ltd.
Rebecca Woods: quoted by permission of Rebecca Woods.

and to the following for permission to include copyright material:

Barratt Homes (BDW Trading Ltd) for extract from David Wilson Homes brochure for Riverside Meadow, Shrewsbury.
Oxford University Press for Word of the Year 2016, at https://en.oxforddictionaries.com/word-of-the-year/word-of-the-year-2016, www.oup.com.
Plain English Campaign: for 'Before and After' from www.plainenglish.co.uk, copyright © Plain English Campaign 2018.
Refugee Action for flyer 'Help a refugee family rebuild their lives: Prem's story'.**Solo Syndication/Associated Newspapers Ltd** for headline from *Daily Mail* front page, 28 March 2017 and three short headlines from *MailOnline*, 27 July 2018.
Telegraph Media Group Ltd (TMG) for screengrab of TMG's *Telegraph.co.uk* containing Robbie Collin: 'Star Wars: The Last Jedi review: thrilling and genuinely startling', 18 Dec 2017, copyright © Telegraph Media Group Ltd 2018.
Vauxhall Motors Ltd for 1933 advertisement, 'For the Big Car Motorist'.

The publisher and authors would like to thank the following for permission to use photographs and other copyright material:

Cover: Nastco/iStockphoto; **p13, 14**: Shutterstock; **p16**: Courtesy of the author; **p46, 47**: Australian Women's Weekly/National Library of Australia; **p64, 66, 67**: Courtesy of the author; **p68**: Shutterstock; **p77**: AP/Shutterstock; **p117**: Oxford University Press; **p135**: Andre Csillag/Shutterstock; **p158**: Archivio Fotografico/123rf; **p161**: Allstar Picture Library/Alamy Stock Photo.

Every effort has been made to contact copyright holders of material reproduced in this book. Any omissions will be rectified in subsequent printings if notice is given to the publisher.

Any third party use of this material, outside of this publication, is prohibited. Interested parties should apply to the copyright holders indicated in each case.

Although we have made every effort to trace and contact all copyright holders before publication this has not been possible in all cases. If notified, the publisher will rectify any errors or omissions at the earliest opportunity.

Key features

These will be included in each chapter.

Key Terms	Definitions of important terminology and concepts
Activities	These will help you develop your skills, knowledge and understanding of important areas of the A level course, allowing you to revise in detail and see the bigger picture
Tip	The tip boxes offer advice about how to approach the questions and tasks that might be set in the examinations
Stretch	These tasks will offer you the chance to find out more details about certain areas and help you read around the course
Transcription key	These keys show features of speech e.g. pauses and simultaneous speech within a transcript

Phonemic alphabet

Phonemic symbols are used throughout this workbook.

single vowels

iː sheep	ɪ ship	ʊ book	uː shoot
e left	ə teacher	ɜː her	ɔː door
æ hat	ʌ up	ɑː far	ɒ on

diphthongs

ɪə here	eɪ wait		
ʊə tourist	ɔɪ coin	əʊ show
eə hair	aɪ like	aʊ mouth

consonants

p pea	b boat	t tree	d dog	tʃ cheese	dʒ joke	k coin	g go
f free	v video	θ thing	ð this	s see	z zoo	ʃ sheep	ʒ television
m mouse	n now	ŋ thing	h hope	l love	r run	w we	j you

What does Paper 1 involve?

Paper 1 lasts 2 hours and 30 minutes and is split into two sections.

Section A: Textual variations and representations

Section A of the Paper 1 exam involves three compulsory questions. You will be given two texts to analyse.

In the exam the pair of texts will always be on broadly the same topic or theme, but you could be given texts from a range of different contexts, including:

- written, spoken or blended in **mode**
- from different **genres**
- for different *purposes*
- aimed at different *audiences*
- from different *times and places*.

The questions will look like this:

> 1. Analyse how **Text A** uses language to create meanings and representations. **[25 marks]**
>
> 2. Analyse how **Text B** uses language to create meanings and representations. **[25 marks]**
>
> 3. Explore the similarities and differences in the ways that **Text A** and **Text B** use language. **[20 marks]**

Section B: Children's language development

In Section B of the Paper 1 exam you have a choice of two questions – Question 4 and Question 5.

One question will be based on children talking (possibly with adults) and one question will be based on children's writing. For both questions, you will be given some data to analyse in relation to a statement that is presented to you concerning children's language. You will be expected to analyse the data, drawing on relevant research and concepts, including your own data and examples where relevant, and using it to form an argument.

Key terms

Genre: In language study, a type of text in any mode which is defined by its purpose, its features, or both. In literary fields, genre tends to refer primarily to the literary genres of prose, poetry and drama, but it can also refer to types of content (for example, crime or romance).

Mode: Speech and writing are called different modes. Digital communication can draw on both of these modes, so is often called a hybrid form of communication.

Here is an example question:

'Interaction with caregivers is the most important influence on a child's language development.'

Referring to **Data Set 1** in detail, and to relevant ideas from language study, evaluate this view of children's language development.　　　**[30 marks]**

How many marks are awarded for each section?

For Section A there are 25 marks for Question 1, 25 marks for Question 2 and 20 marks for Question 3.

For Section B there are 30 marks for either Question 4 or Question 5 (whichever you choose to answer).

How long should you spend on each section?

You should spend roughly 30 minutes reading and preparing the texts. In Section A, you should then spend roughly 30 minutes writing your Question 1 response, 30 minutes for Question 2 and 20 minutes for Question 3.

For Section B, spend roughly 40 minutes writing up your answer.

How is Section A assessed?

Questions 1 and 2

- AO1: 10 marks – You must analyse the texts applying the appropriate language methods, using precise terminology and coherent written expression.

- AO3: 15 marks – Your analysis should always be led by **meanings** and **representations**. You must analyse and evaluate how contextual factors and language features connect with the construction of meaning.

Question 3

- AO4: 20 marks – You must explore connections across the texts, and this must be informed by linguistic concepts and methods.

How is Section B assessed?

- AO1: 15 marks – You must carefully analyse the data using appropriate methods of language analysis and using accurate linguistic terminology.

- AO2: 15 marks – You must demonstrate a critical understanding of concepts and issues relevant to language use. You must show a clear understanding of the issues surrounding children's language and evaluate different approaches to the topic. You should evaluate the issues in light of the data given.

> **Key terms**
>
> **Meanings:** Messages that are communicated. Meanings are never fixed, but are negotiated between speakers (or writers) and listeners (or readers), and vary considerably according to context.
>
> **Representation:** Something that stands in place of something else. Representation is how something *appears* to be, not how it really *is*.

Tip

It is vital that you get to grips with what each text means and how those meanings are created through language choices. To be successful in these questions, you will need to balance the bigger picture of each text with closely focused detail. When you get to Question 3, you will need to explore what makes the texts similar and/or different.

How to analyse texts for A level English Language

Introduction

One of your main tasks in the A level course is to analyse texts of all types, exploring how they create meanings and representations. You will already have done a lot of this type of work in your course, so in the first few chapters of this revision workbook you will look at some key approaches that are particularly useful for the Paper 1 exam. Later in this workbook you will see how many of the same approaches can be used on Paper 2 as well, so bear this in mind.

This workbook will help you to understand what is rewarded on the mark scheme and how this might have an impact on how you approach the task. This chapter will start with very short revision tasks based on text extracts, then work towards longer, more developed activities, before finishing with exam-style paired text tasks. Along the way, you will see how the Assessment Objectives operate. You will also be given a range of different kinds of texts to prepare you for the exam.

What does it mean?

Activity 1

1. Look at the text extracts below and on page 9 and try to summarise, in one short sentence, what you think the main meanings are. What kinds of texts are they and what contexts might have produced them? What views, ideas and attitudes do you think are being communicated?

   a.

   > The food was – bizarrely – both under-cooked and over-fried, with the tempura prawns still frozen in the middle yet frazzled to a crisp on the outside. Some achievement.

   _____

   _____

   b.

   > it was the most frightened that I have **ev**er been (.)
   > I **lit**erally could not move and I just kind of stood there thinking (.) why am I even getting on this ride

   Transcription key

   (.)   normal pause
   bold   indicates a stressed syllable

   _____

   _____

Key terms

Discourse: A stretch of language (spoken, written or **multimodal**) considered in its context of use. The plural use of the term – discourses – refers to repeated ways of talking or writing about a topic.

Grammar: The structural aspects of language that tie items together. Grammar includes syntax, or word order; and morphology, or the elements added to words to show their grammatical role (such as '-ed' to indicate the past tense of a verb).

c.

> Yeah went ok I suppose but cant help feel I couldve done a bit more preparation for it but y'know...we'll see.

_____

_____

2. Now try to identify exactly which words, phrases and other language features help create these meanings. Circle the most important words that create these meanings. You will return to these later in this chapter.

Representation

Language is used to create meanings, but on another level it also creates representations, in the sense that all language somehow represents the world to us in a particular way. One way to approach representations is to look at a text and consider how the following are represented to us:

- events
- people
- issues
- opinions
- actions
- ideas
- feelings
- identities.

The individual meanings of certain language choices often fit together to create a particular perspective or version of events. At the higher levels of the mark scheme, examiners are looking for students who can see what these representations are and how they have been created through language.

Language analysis

The other key aspect of language analysis is describing linguistically the language devices used to create meanings. AO1 marks are awarded for both _detail_ and _range_. Remind yourself of the language levels used throughout this course in the table below.

Lexis and **semantics**	Word choices and their meanings
Graphology	Layout and visual design
Syntax	Part of **grammar**: word order and structure
Phonology	How sounds are analysed in language
Discourse	A stretch of language (spoken, written or multimodal)
Pragmatics	The implied meanings of language
Morphology	The internal structure of words themselves

Key terms

Graphology: All the visual aspects of textual design, including colour, typeface, layout, images and logos.

Lexis: The vocabulary of a language.

Morphology: The aspect of grammar that refers to grammatical markings. For example, the 's' ending on nouns can indicate a plural form (one book, two books).

Multimodal: A multimodal text employs more than one mode of communication – for example, by using images as well as words, or by drawing on an aspect of speech as well as writing.

Phonetics / Phonology: The study of the sound system. Phonetics refers to the physical production and reception of sound, while phonology is a more abstract idea about all the sounds of a particular language.

Pragmatics: The study of how words are used in a particular context to create a certain meaning.

Semantics: The meanings of words and expressions. Semantics can also refer to meaning in a broader sense, i.e. the overall meaning of something.

Syntax: How words are arranged, or the word order that is typical of a language.

When analysing texts, you will need to make use of the most appropriate language levels to explain how language has been used and to provide the most appropriate labels for the features used.

The 'performance characteristics' on the mark scheme remain the same each year, while the 'indicative content' changes from year to year and question to question, depending on the actual texts set; however, it follows a recognisable structure for AO1.

- Level 1: minimal understanding of how language works

- Level 2: the beginnings of analysis but lacking detail, precision and depth

- Level 3: this is where you start to show detailed engagement with language, describing **salient** language features of different kinds

- Level 4: more detail and range in your language analysis, showing understanding of different aspects of language

- Level 5: all of these together with a grasp of the most complex and demanding uses of language and how patterns of language have been shaped

Key terms

Adjective / Adjectival: Adjectives give more information about nouns, describing the qualities of people and things.

Adverb / Adverbial: Adverbs give more information about verbs – typically, where, when and in what manner the action of the verb takes place. Adverbial elements can be phrases, so aren't necessarily single words.

Antonym: A word that means the opposite.

Salient: Most important.

Semantic pattern: A cluster of words with similar uses.

Activity 2

Go back to your notes on the three examples from Activity 1 on pages 8–9. You were asked to circle the words, phrases and other language features that were important for constructing meanings in each text.

Below are some examples of the kind of AO1 work you might be able to do on some of the significant parts of each example. Compare these with the detail you identified.

a.

> The food was – bizarrely – both under-cooked and over-fried, with the tempura prawns still frozen in the middle yet frazzled to a crisp on the outside. Some achievement.

- *bizarrely* – The **adverb** is inserted to create the sense that this is a strange situation.

- *under-cooked and over-fried* – A semantic contrast is created with the **antonyms** under- and over-.

- *frozen* and *frazzled* – These two **adjectives** contrast two different states of cooking and help to establish a kind of **semantic pattern** with the example above.

- *Some achievement.* – A minor sentence acts as a brief comment and evaluation on the previous description.

b.

> it was the most frightened that I have **ev**er been (.)
> I **lit**erally could not move and I just kind of stood there
> thinking (.) why am I even getting on this ride

- *ever* – The adverb of time seems to add an extra degree of power to the expression of fear.

- *literally* – The metaphorical adverb (often used to mean 'figuratively') acts to amplify the inability to move.

- *I just kind of stood there* – The spoken mode makes use of different aspects of language and here the **hedge** *kind of* suggests a slightly vague description.

- *why am I even getting on this ride* – The speaker's choice to quote her own thoughts in an **interrogative clause** helps to bring the situation to life, creating a voice to represent the fear felt about the ride.

c.

> Yeah went ok I suppose but cant help feel
> I couldve done a bit more preparation for
> it but y'know…we'll see.

- *I suppose* – This comment clause is inserted to offer a sense of doubt or reflection on what has been said and what might be to come.

- *Yeah went ok I suppose but cant help feeling* – The fact that the text is from a form of **computer-mediated communication (CMC)** means that abbreviated grammatical structures can be used to save time, so the **subject** ellipses (leaving out the subject of each clause: *It went ok… I can't help feeling*) are examples of this. This is less to do with the meanings created by the language choices and more to do with the context the language is produced in.

- *but y'know…we'll see* – These are quite casual expressions, perhaps more familiar in spoken discourse. *Y'know* acts as a kind of confirmation check or address to the reader, although might also just be a filler. *We'll see* offers a brief, rather vague, evaluation and leaves the ending open.

Key terms

Computer-mediated communication (CMC): Human communication that takes place via the medium of computers.

Hedge: Cautious language used to make what we say less direct or certain.

Interrogative clause: A question.

Subject: The thing or person carrying out the action of a verb.

Bringing it together: using 'hotspots'

Now you have looked at short text extracts, it's time to think a little more about an approach to analysing whole texts and then exploring the similarities and differences between them for Question 3. Here is one suggested approach.

- Read the two texts you are given for meaning, making notes on what each text is about, and what is being said about the topic.

- Make sure you have a clear overview of each text. Is the material represented from one viewpoint or many? Are there different ideas within the texts that you might want to consider (for example, different speakers or writers who are offering different views or talking about different things)?

- Find five or six 'hotspots' in each text. These are areas in each text that convey the clearest and most useful ideas. These hotspots could be a single phrase, a section of the text (an image, a headline, the opening or closing lines), a sentence or even a pattern of language across the whole text. These hotspots should *mean something* and, in some cases at least, represent the topic or views on the topic in a way that you can analyse in real detail. These need to be salient; it's vital to get to grips with language that means something and contributes to the overall meanings in each text.

- Analyse the language in these hotspots that is used to create these meanings. Think about the different language levels and use precise AO1 terms, making sure you are offering a good range across each text. AO1 is not *just* about grammatical labels (word classes, phrases, sentences, clauses, **tense**, etc.), but it is also about things like **semantic fields**, patterns of meaning (contrast, **antithesis** and juxtaposition, for example), graphology, interaction patterns (especially in spoken texts or ones using features of spoken language), **discourse structure**, pragmatics and perhaps phonology in some texts too.

- There will be many different ways to do this and if you've selected meaningful parts of the texts, you'll be able to explain them effectively. Examiners don't really want to read about a text having 'lots of long sentences to make it flow' or 'lots of **pronouns** to make it personal' because these are meaningless generalisations. Look closely at what is actually meant in each text *in its given context*.

- While analysing these hotspots, keep in mind the bigger picture of what each text is doing and what kind of texts they are. You will need to address these issues a bit more in your answer to Question 3, but they will also be useful in Questions 1 and 2. For example, if the text is typical of a particular genre, you know it will generally do certain things (for example, recipes tell you what to do, stories recount events).

- Another important aspect to consider is not just how the topic of each text is represented but how the text creators (writers, speakers, posters, texters and so on) represent themselves and each other. How do they position themselves in relation to the text receivers? How do they present a face or image to the audience and to each other? How does this relate to what the texts are about?

- As you are making notes on these aspects of each text, you should also be looking to group together various points for Question 3. Given that each text is on the same topic, how is each text handling that topic? How relevant are the different contexts to each text?

Key terms

Antithesis: A person or thing that is the direct opposite.

Discourse structure: The internal structure of a text.

Pronoun: Pronouns can stand in place of nouns, hence the term 'pro-noun'. Standard English personal pronouns are: I, you, he, she, it, and one (singular); we, you and they (plural).

Semantic field: A group of terms from the same domain. For example, names for food or aspects of computer communication.

Tense: The way in which verbs can indicate time, for example the '-ed' ending on a verb such as 'look' indicates past time.

The capitalisation, larger font size and exclamation mark helps to draw attention to this imperative headline, assisting in its persuasive function.

ADOPT AN ENDANGERED ANIMAL TODAY!

By adopting an endangered animal, you will be helping to save them from extinction. You will be playing an important part in helping us to protect these animals and their habitats.

If you adopt an animal you will receive:
- regular updates about how your animal is getting on
- our quarterly magazine, giving you fun facts about a range of animals
- a cute cuddly toy to be cherished forever

The emotive language such as the alliterative adjectival phrase 'cute cuddly' and the participle phrase 'cherished forever' helps with the persuasive function.

"I feel so happy that I have helped a Black Rhino and I take my cuddly rhino everywhere with me"
Evie-May, 6

THESE ARE SOME OF OUR BEST-LOVED ANIMALS
AND THEY NEED YOUR HELP TODAY.

The visual design of the charity advert is important and the bullet points help organise the information, demonstrating the benefits of adopting an animal to the text receiver.

The image of the girl is linked to a section that appears to have been spoken by her in the first person, creating a new voice in the text and another way of persuading the reader.

How to annotate a text in the exam identifying 'hotspots'

You could be faced with any kind of written, spoken or electronic text in Section A of the Paper 1 exam, so you need to ensure you have had plenty of practice analysing a variety of different texts. In this chapter, you will look at revision approaches to analysing written texts.

In Questions 1 and 2 you will need to consider the meanings of the texts in their contexts. In Question 3 you will need to explore the similarities and differences between the two texts, which means that you will need to consider most or all of the following:

- mode – whether the texts are written, spoken or multimodal

- genre – the type of text and how each might be categorised

- audience – who each text is aimed at, or appears to be aimed at (the text receivers)

- purpose – what each text is designed to do

- time and place – the age of each text and where it comes from.

As outlined earlier, it is vital to get to grips early on with what each text is about and how language is being used within it to create meanings and representations. As there are 15 marks for AO3 and 10 for AO1, it makes sense to take an AO3-led approach to text in Section A. This means that you should root your analysis in the texts in front of you and the various contexts that have contributed to them. It also makes sense to start with a clear grasp of the bigger picture of each text before moving into the language details.

Activity 1

Read each of the extracts on pages 14–16 and answer the questions that follow them, annotating the texts to highlight hotspots (as outlined in the previous chapter) to support your observations.

Text A is from a wildlife charity campaign leaflet.

Text A

The pictures are a part of the language too (graphology) and they help represent two different images of the animals – a realistic one of the animal in the natural world and a child's soft toy version, perhaps appealing to two different audiences.

The Black Rhino, native to Eastern and Southern Africa, is critically endangered so needs your help. Its double horned head is its unique feature. If you adopt a Black Rhino, you will be helping to protect it from the threat of hunters and poachers.

Here's your opportunity to adopt one of the cutest animals on the planet: the Giant Panda. Endangered since 1990, the Panda is the symbol of peace in China and is instantly recognisable due to its distinctive eyespots, which are shaped like teardrops.

You could adopt the vulnerable Siberian Tiger. Did you know that there are only around 500 Siberian Tigers left in the wild? Desperately under threat from habitat loss and poaching, will you help these animals secure their future?

Text A represents pandas as 'one of the cutest animals on the planet', emphasising their popularity with the superlative adjective 'cutest'. They are also represented as being under threat using the adverbial 'endangered since 1990'.

1. How are black rhinos being represented in Text A?

_____

_____

_____

2. What language choices have been made to create these representations?

_____

_____

_____

_____

3. What purposes and audiences do you think the text producers have in mind and how do these contribute to the language choices being made?

_____

_____

_____

_____

_____

Text B is from a brochure advertising new houses in Shrewsbury.

Text B

Blessed with many traditional independently owned shops – from hatters and ironmongers to delicatessens and designer boutiques – Shrewsbury also has a sociable and exceptionally friendly café society, with contemporary bars and restaurants sitting comfortably alongside traditional pubs and cosy tea-shops. Culture is also high on the Shrewsbury agenda, with a vigorous programme of all-year-round theatre and live events, plus a summer Arts Festival – and a famous Flower Show, one of the biggest in the country.

Text B represents Shrewsbury as having a mixture of 'traditional' and 'contemporary' attractions for people who live there. These adjective choices present a town with a sense of history but also an up-to-date atmosphere.

4. How is the town of Shrewsbury being represented in Text B?

_____

_____

_____

_____

_____

5. What language choices have been made to create these representations?

_____

_____

_____

_____

6. What purposes and audiences do you think the text producers have in mind and how do these contribute to the language choices being made?

_____

_____

_____

_____

_____

Text C is from a board outside a coffee shop.

Text C

Text C directly addresses its ideal audience of coffee drinkers with an interrogative and second person pronoun, setting up the whole structure of the text as something that follows from this question.

7. How is coffee being represented and how does the coffee shop business represent itself?

_____

_____

_____

_____

8. What type of text is this and who is the ideal audience?

_____

_____

_____

9. What are the purposes of Text C?

_____

_____

_____

_____

Contexts

All texts, whatever their source, have some kind of context. They don't exist in a vacuum because they will all have been produced by a person (or people) to fulfil a communicative need and have been designed with an audience in mind.

All texts have a purpose and many texts have multiple purposes. Often these texts can be grouped together because they perform similar roles. It is important to consider what a text is designed to do by the text producers because this will often dictate some of the language choices made.

Audience is also very important to consider because texts are often designed to be read by a specific person or group of people.

A connected aspect of text analysis is to consider what type of text you are analysing. One way to think about written texts is to consider the genre they belong to and how this influences the language choices made. The genre a text belongs to will often give you some useful starting points for analysis in Questions 1 and 2, but can also allow you to explore the similarities and differences between the pair of texts for Question 3.

A final concept that is important here is mode. The texts in this chapter all make use of the written mode and it is therefore helpful to consider what the written mode offers that the spoken (and, to some extent, electronic) mode might not.

You will move on to look at time and place as other contextual factors later in this chapter.

Genre is often connected to what a text is designed to do (its purpose) and who it is aimed at (audience). Before you start to look in more detail at what a text is actually about, you might want to consider these aspects and think about how they can shape the meanings as well.

Activity 2

Copy and complete the table below by identifying the types of texts that could come under the categories listed in the first column. Some examples have been given but add your own, too. Then complete the third column and outline the characteristic **generic** features of those types of texts. You could choose to produce mind maps for each text type. Think about all language levels.

Purposes	Types of texts	Characteristic style features
Texts that persuade	Opinion articles	**Rhetorical** devices, for example:
Texts that inform	Guide books	
Texts that instruct or advise		Grammatical choices to instruct, for example:
Texts that entertain	Comic books	

Tip

While it is important to think about the characteristic style features when you read and analyse a text, it is equally important that you actually get to grips with the text there in front of you. Don't assume that just because a text is of a certain genre it will automatically have certain features. Look for what is in the text and what that tells you.

It is important to remember that texts can have multiple purposes just as they can have multiple audiences; they rarely just inform or instruct or entertain or persuade. For example, texts that entertain may seek to persuade readers to think in particular ways. Texts that advise may also inform the reader at the same time. In addition, a text may appear to be addressed towards a sense of a constructed 'ideal' reader, but real readers will often be very different from that. Discussions of audience should cover both, where possible.

Activity 3

1. Read Text D, part of a campaign by the charity Refugee Action, which calls on readers to support people who have been forced to flee their homes. Answer the following questions on a separate piece of paper.

   a. Who do you think is the target audience for Text D?

   b. What genre would you place this text in?

    c. How does this text represent Prem and his family's experiences?

    d. How does it persuade people to support the campaign?

    e. How do the choices of graphology, semantics, discourse structure and grammar work to reinforce the purposes of the text and the representations it constructs?

2. Now, on separate paper, use your answers to write an analysis of this text, addressing the following exam-style question:

> Analyse how **Text D** uses language to create meanings and representations.
>
> **[25 marks]**

Text D

PREM'S STORY

Prem is a Bhutanese refugee who has been resettled through Refugee Action's programme. He arrived in the UK with his family in 2010, from a UN refugee camp in Nepal where he had lived for almost 20 years.

When he was still a child his family fled violence in neighbouring Bhutan, and there was no going back. He went to school in that refugee camp, but as a refugee in Nepal he could never work. He and his family lived in a hut, and were fed on standard rations. Prem got married and had two daughters but his life was in limbo, living in basic, miserable conditions, with no way to do anything for himself or his family.

Once in the UK, Refugee Action supported Prem and his family through the first year. Everything was unfamiliar. The bureaucracy, the money, shopping. Getting registered with a doctor, and the children into school. Refugee Action helped Prem get on training courses that enabled him to find work, and helped him and his wife find English classes.

Five years after arriving in the UK, Prem works two jobs. He passed accountancy exams and does some bookkeeping, and also works in a care home. His young children are 'very English' now, he says, but he and his wife are concerned that they learn about their own culture, and are involved in a Bhutanese cultural group.

Analysing structure

Written texts often make use of different structures. As you can see from the Refugee Action text (Text D), part of the leaflet involves telling Prem's story. Look at the ways in which the narrative is constructed using different language devices and techniques to sequence the events that have taken place and the times when they occurred.

Some of these are:

- use of different tenses – present ('Prem works two jobs') and past ('his family fled violence')

- use of adverbials – clauses ('When he was still a child…'), prepositional phrases ('in 2010'), **noun phrases** ('almost 20 years').

Beginning to examine older texts

While the texts you analyse in the exam might be selected from any genre or mode, be aimed at any target audience, and be for any purpose, you know that one of them (Text B in the exam) will always be an older text (as far back as 1600, potentially).

In the texts you have looked at so far, you have not been asked specifically about time as a factor. How relevant might it be to each text? Which language choices and meanings might be linked to the age of each text? Sometimes this is easier to see in older texts where the vocabulary, grammar or graphology might appear unfamiliar, but it is also worth considering with modern texts.

Activity 4

Text E opposite is a car advertisement from 1933. Read the text and make notes on separate paper, about the ways in which time might be a factor in how this text uses language to represent its subject matter, address its audience and achieve its purpose. Use the following headings to organise your notes as you look at the different aspects of it:

- audience

- purpose

- genre

- mode

- time

- how the subject is represented

- linguistic analysis.

Make sure that you identify some key hotspots to analyse in more detail – you can annotate the text as you work. You will return to this text in the chapter *Paper 1, Section A: Comparing texts* (pages 44–48), so keep your notes handy.

Text E

FOR THE BIG CAR MOTORIST

. . . amazing moneysworth !

This big, luxurious Vauxhall Saloon

£325

TAX ONLY £15

Vauxhall Big Six Models, 5-Seater Saloon £325, Tickford Foursome Drophead Coupé £365, Wingham Convertible Cabriolet £395. For those who prefer higher power and even more outstanding performance the above models are available with a 27-h.p. engine at no extra charge. Tax £20 5s.

7-seater Limousine on Vauxhall Six Size Long 10 ft. 10 in. Wheelbase chassis (27-h.p. engine only). Coachwork by Grosvenor £550.

ON PERFORMANCE, comfort, and appearance alone the Vauxhall Big Six holds its own against any other big car of its type in the world, yet this full five-seater Saloon costs only £325. It has the coachwork quality and finish associated with the most exclusive productions, thoughtfully selected equipment and engineering features not to be found on much more expensive cars—entirely automatic chassis lubrication, pedomatic starting, vacuum-controlled ignition, Synchro-Mesh gears, self-returning direction indicators and Vauxhall No-Draught Ventilation. On the road it is delightful to drive, answering the controls eagerly, soaring away into real speed when the throttle is opened. In short, the Vauxhall Box Six is a big car fit for service anywhere, the latest embodiment of a tradition of which is makers are justly proud, and selling at a price only made possible by the exceptional manufacturing resourced of the famous Vauxhall factory at Luton.

VAUXHALL BIG SIX

CAN NOW BE SEEN AND TRIED AT ALL VAUXHALL DEALERS

or London Showrooms, 174-182 Great Portland Street, W.1. Catalogue on request from Vauxhall Motors Ltd., Edgware Rd., The Hyde, London, N.W.9.

Exploring other kinds of written texts

Alongside texts that persuade, inform and tell stories, you might find texts that offer opinions and views. The text below and continuing on page 22, is a review of the film *Psycho*, published in *The Observer* in 1960.

Text F

Psycho: Archive review

From *The Observer*, 7 August 1960

A new film by Alfred Hitchcock is usually a keen enjoyment. *Psycho* turns out to be an exception. The story, adapted from a novel by Robert Bloch, has to do with the fate of one Marion (Janet Leigh), an uninhibited secretary, who steals $40,000 from her employer and drives off into the night to meet her lover (John Gavin). During a storm she arrives at a sinister motel owned by a crazy taxidermist (Anthony Perkins), whose even more demented mother lives in the adjoining mansion.

There follows one of the most disgusting murders in all screen history. It takes place in a bathroom and involves a great deal of swabbing of the tiles and flushings of the lavatory. It might be described with fairness as plug ugly. *Psycho* is not a long film but it feels long. Perhaps because the director dawdles over technical effects; perhaps because it is difficult, if not impossible, to care about any of the characters.

The stupid air of mystery and portent surrounding *Psycho*'s presentation strikes me as a tremendous error. "The manager of this theatre has been instructed, at the risk of his life, not to admit any persons after the picture starts. By the way, after you see *Psycho* don't give away the ending." Signed, Alfred Hitchcock.

I couldn't give away the ending if I wanted to, for the simple reason that I grew so sick and tired of the whole beastly business that I didn't stop to see it. Your edict may keep me out of the theatre, my dear Hitchcock, but I'm hanged if it will keep me in.

Tip

One of the best ways to ensure you are ready for different texts in the exam is to read a range of different genres and practise analysing them. Go through the different text types and genres from Activity 2 earlier and find examples to use for practice.

Activity 5

1. Circle key hotspots within Text F that you think are crucial to its overall meanings.

2. On separate paper, write a short analysis of this text, focusing on the ways in which the writer has used language to express opinions and put forward ideas about the film. As you write, try to integrate discussion of meaning or representations with close reference to the text. This will help you link AO3 with your detailed AO1 language analysis. You will need to use this text again in the chapter *Paper 1, Section A: Comparing texts* (pages 44–48), so keep your notes handy.

When you analyse texts in the exam, you will need to consider:

- the different positions adopted
- the perspectives offered
- the ways in which language shapes different representations.

Activity 6

Text G opposite is an eyewitness account of the 'Peterloo massacre' of 1819 where a peaceful protest in Manchester was attacked by British soldiers who killed 18 people and injured hundreds. Read the text and carry out the tasks below on separate paper. You will need to use this text again in the chapter *Paper 1, Section A: Comparing texts* (pages 44–48) so keep your notes handy.

1. Write a short overview (two or three sentences) of Text G in which you summarise the main points made by the writer and the version of events he is expressing.

2. Explain how the writer has used his own eyewitness perspective to represent events.

3. Which hotspots would you use as part of a detailed analysis of Text G? Start to annotate the four or five areas you have identified.

Text G

In about half an hour after our arrival the sounds of music and reiterated shouts proclaimed the near approach of Mr. Hunt and his party; and in a minute or two they were seen coming from Deansgate, preceded by a band of music and several flags. [...] Their approach was hailed by one universal shout from probably eighty thousand persons. They threaded their way slowly past us and through the crowd, which Hunt eyed, I thought, with almost as much of astonishment as satisfaction. This spectacle could not be otherwise in his view than solemnly impressive. Such a mass of human beings he had not beheld till then. His responsibility must weigh on his mind. [...] The task was great, and not without its peril. The meeting was indeed a tremendous one. [...] Mr. Hunt, stepping towards the front of the stage, took off his white hat, and addressed the people.

[...] we had got to nearly the outside of the crowd, when a noise and strange murmur arose towards the church. Some persons said it was the Blackburn people coming; and I stood on tip-toe and looked in the direction whence the noise proceeded, and saw a party of cavalry in blue and white uniform come trotting, sword in hand, round the corner of a garden-wall, and to the front of a row of new houses, where they reined up in a line.

'The soldiers are here,' I said; 'we must go back and see what this means.' 'Oh,' someone made reply, 'they are only come to be ready if there should be any disturbance in the meeting.' 'Well, let us go back,' I said, and we forced our way towards the colours.

On the cavalry drawing up they were received with a shout of good-will, as I understood it. They shouted again, waving their sabres over their heads; and then, slackening rein, and striking spur into their steeds, they dashed forward and began cutting the people.

'Stand fast,' I said, 'they are riding upon us; stand fast'. [...] The cavalry were in confusion: they evidently could not, with all the weight of man and horse, penetrate that compact mass of human beings; and their sabres were plied to hew a way through naked held-up hands and defenceless heads; and then chopped limbs and wound-gaping skulls were seen; and groans and cries were mingled with the din of that horrid confusion. [...]

Many females appeared as the crowd opened; and striplings or mere youths also were found. Their cries were piteous and heart-rending, and would, one might have supposed, have disarmed any human resentment: but here their appeals were in vain. [...]

In ten minutes from the commencement of the havoc the field was an open and almost deserted space. The sun looked down through a sultry and motionless air. The curtains and blinds of the windows within view were all closed. [...] The hustings remained, with a few broken and hewed flag-staves erect, and a torn and gashed banner or two dropping; whilst over the whole field were strewed caps, bonnets, hats, shawls, and shoes, and other parts of male and female dress, trampled, torn, and bloody. [...] Several mounds of human being still remained where they had fallen, crushed down and smothered. Some of these still groaning, others with staring eyes, were gasping for breath, and others would never breathe more. All was silent save those low sounds, and the occasional snorting and pawing of steeds.

Key terms

Colloquial: Colloquial expressions are items of everyday language used in informal contexts.

Formal / Formality: Designed for use on serious or public occasions where people pay attention to behaviour and appearance.

Intonation: Tunes, created from variations in pitch, that convey meaning in the speech of a particular language.

Prosodics / Prosody: Prosody is the melody that our voices create via prosodic aspects such as rhythm and **intonation**.

Transcript: A record of what speakers said and did.

The speech context

As part of your preparation for Paper 1, Section A, you will have studied the features of spoken language and you will have analysed a range of **transcripts**. As with any textual analysis, it is essential that you consider what is being said and how the topic is being represented. Context has a big impact on the language we use. For example, the spoken language we use in a **formal** presentation will be very different from the spoken language we use when chatting to our friends.

AO3 requires you to carefully examine how contextual factors work together with language features to create meanings, so it is really important that you consider and understand all the background factors that impact on *what* is being said and *how* it is being said.

There are numerous factors which influence an individual's language choices in conversation and how he or she conducts that conversation. Contextual factors could include things such as:

• the situation – where the speakers are, the time of day, how comfortable they feel in that situation
• the participants – the level of familiarity between the speakers
• the degree of spontaneity
• roles and status of the speakers – how the power is distributed
• the purpose of the exchange
• the topic and degree of familiarity with that topic
• the age of the speakers
• the attitudes and feelings of the speakers
• the social and cultural values of the speakers.

> **Tip**
>
> It is important to be mindful that AO3 is worth 15 out of a possible 25 marks for each of Questions 1 and Question 2. This means that it is essential that you read the texts for meaning *first* and that you jot down as many notes as you can on context, meanings and representations.

Activity 1

Consider the following three scenarios. Think about the most important factors that may impact on the language used and jot them down in note form. Then consider the language choices we may expect the speakers to make and jot these down underneath. Some notes have been made on the first one to help you. Complete the tables for Scenarios 2 and 3 yourself.

Scenario 1: Two Manchester United supporters on the football terraces
Contextual factors that may affect language use: • How well the participants know one other   • Whether Manchester United are winning or losing   • The atmosphere and attitude of other supporters in the ground

- The importance of the match (for example, FA Cup final or pre-season friendly)
- The ongoing action on the pitch
- The use of communication tools (for example, mobile phones, display boards)
- The physical behaviour of others in the crowd

Typical language features that we may expect from this type of exchange:

- Emphasised **prosodic** features, for example, shouting, chanting, singing
- Non-verbal features, for example, head in hands, pointing, frowning, smiling
- Informal, **colloquial** language
- Language relating to the semantic field of football
- Some simultaneous speech

Scenario 2: A 16-year-old being interviewed for her first part-time job

Contextual factors that may affect language use:

Typical language features that we may expect from this type of exchange (make notes on the use of language by both the interviewer and the interviewee):

Scenario 3: Strangers on a first date after meeting on Tinder

Contextual factors that may affect language use:

Typical language features that we may expect from this type of exchange:

Key terms

First language (L1): The first language learned by an individual, usually in childhood.

Non-standard: Different from normal or majority usage.

The spoken text that you may be faced with in Section A of the Paper 1 exam could consist of a variety of data types. Speech can be:

- spontaneous
- planned
- semi-spontaneous.

It is essential that you understand the type of speech that you are faced with and the typical features of that genre.

Tip

Always pay close attention to non-fluency features and why they are used in a situation. For example, non-fluency features are normal features of discourse. However, heavy use of non-fluency features could show, for example, that a speaker is nervous, excited or even angry, or it could demonstrate that the person's **first language** is not English. It is important to analyse the context and then decide what the language features may be demonstrating or whether they are simply expected features of that mode.

Activity 2

Create a mind map of the features of spontaneous discourse below:

Features of spontaneous speech

Activity 3

Complete the following table.

1. Identify the type of each spoken text in the second column.

2. Jot down some notes in the third column to describe some key characteristics of that genre. If it is a two-way exchange, consider the language of both speakers.

The first row has been done for you.

Spoken text	Spontaneous, planned or semi-spontaneous?	Key characteristics
The Channel 4 evening news	Planned	– Carefully edited, scripted speech – An organised discourse structure – Prosodic emphasis to draw attention to key sections – Discourse markers to signal the beginning of the next news item – Avoiding **non-standard** English
An extract from *The Jeremy Kyle Show*		
A teacher being interviewed for a promotion		
An argument between two friends		
A parent telling a child to go to bed		

Activity 4

Consider the following snippets of conversation, all of which were heard on a bus and were spoken by different people. Think about how each speaker represents the topic, other people, places and ideas. Complete the table that follows. Consider using some of the terms below the table to analyse the data linguistically.

a. yeah it's annoying being veggie because when I order curry (.), I have to order the meat one and take all the meat out (.) it's a total pain (.) if only people respected that some of us don't want to murder animals

b. but hummus (.) when did that happen (.) there's a restaurant down the road and that's all they do (.) but that isn't a proper meal it's a side order innit, it's like having a restaurant just flogging tomato ketchup (.) what a rubbish idea (.) it's never gonna work

c. every time I tell people I took BTEC Performing Arts and Drama they look at me like I'm incompetent or something (.) like A levels are oh so superior (.) so pretentious

> **Transcription key**
>
> (.)   normal pause

Quotation from the data	Notes about meanings and representations	Linguistic terms to analyse the quotation
'it's annoying being veggie because when I order curry… I have to take all the meat out'		
'it's a total pain'		
'if only people respected that some of us don't want to murder animals'		
'hummus… that isn't a proper meal it's a side order innit'		
'what a rubbish idea (.) it's never gonna work'		
'they look at me like I'm incompetent or something'		

Quotation from the data	Notes about meanings and representations	Linguistic terms to analyse the quotation
'like A levels are oh so superior'		
'so pretentious'		

vague language	an intensifier	a clipping	elision
an **initialism**	an abstract noun phrase	a violent dynamic verb	
a subordinate clause	a colloquial tag question	an evaluative post-modifying adjective	

Talking on the phone

You could be given any kind of spoken text in the exam, including transcripts of conversations. The more practice you have reading and annotating different types of data, the more prepared you will be for the exam.

> **Key term**
>
> **Initialism:** Initials that cannot be pronounced as words (e.g. DVD).

Activity 5

Read the transcripts on page 30 of some messages left on Grace's voicemail.

Answer the following questions for each of the messages, using a separate piece of paper. You could also annotate the data to show the different contextual factors that may impact on the language used in the different messages.

1. What is the purpose of each of the messages?

2. Can you make any assumptions about roles and relationships between the speakers and Grace?

3. Are each of these messages planned or spontaneous? How do you know?

4. How does the medium of the telephone affect the language used?

5. Are there any differences in the formality of the messages? Why and how?

> **Tip**
>
> As you have seen, AO1 tests your ability to apply appropriate language terminology to the data in a carefully expressed, accurate way. It is important to understand that AO1 works hand in hand with AO3, so you need to have something of worth to say about a feature and you must avoid simply spotting features with no discussion.

Transcription key

(.)   normal pause

- hiya (.) it's just me (.) I'm leaving work now (.) as long as the traffic's ok I should be back in an hour and a bit (.) hope the kids haven't driven you up the wall today (.) love yer

- this is a message for Miss (.) Wooldridge (.) erm we've noticed from our records that your MOT is due by (.) erm (.) sorry (.) I had the date here (.) yes (.) the twenty seventh of August (.) so (.) could you please get in touch with us at Church Street Motors if you'd like to get your car booked in (.) thanks

- hi hun (.) it's only me (.) so sorry but I'm not gonna be able to make drinks tonight (.) Izzy's been spewing for like (.) the past few hours so (.) erm (.) sorry again (.) was really looking forward to it as well (.) speak soon

- morning (.) it's Mandy here (.) from work (.) yeah (.) I've noticed that you erm (.) you didn't leave that report on my desk (.) erm the report from accounts (.) please could you get back to me (.) thanks (.) bye now

Activity 6

Look back at the voicemail data in Activity 5 above and identify an example of each of the linguistic features below. While the data is one-way communication, people often draw on the conventions of two-way speech in this context. Think about how this adds to the meanings created. Copy and complete the following table.

Feature	Quotation	Analysis – what is the effect of this use of language? How does it create meanings and representations?
Transactional talk (talk which focuses on getting something done)		
Interactional talk (where the emphasis is on the social relationship between the speakers)		
The use of contractions		
The use of elision		
The use of slang		
An endearing address term		
A mitigated directive		
The use of fillers		
Politeness markers		

Power, roles and relationships

When we speak, we not only represent people, places, ideas, and so on, but we also represent ourselves: we construct our identities. These identities can, of course, change. For example, sometimes we may wish to show ourselves as hard-working, studious individuals, whereas other times we may want to show ourselves as fun, carefree risk-takers. We have the ability to move between styles of speech without even thinking about it. This is known as style-shifting.

Activity 7

Read the four scenarios in Text A below. Jo, a 37-year-old female, is a teacher and is married with two young children.

Think about the changing role of Jo, and the linguistic features that reveal Jo's status in the exchanges. Annotate the data with your ideas.

Exam technique: remember to first identify contextual factors (AO3) and then apply the linguistic methods and terminology (AO1).

Use these questions to help with your annotations.

- What is the purpose of each of the exchanges?

- Who is involved and what is the role and status of each speaker?

- What factors influence the relationships?

- How is the relationship between the speakers demonstrated through the language used?

Text A

Scenario 1: Jo is at home – 7.30am. Seb is Jo's seven-year-old son.

J: come on Seb (.) it's time to get your coat on

S: but I don't want to go to school

J: come on sweetheart (.) we don't want to be late

S: no (.) I don't want to

J: hurry up and get your coat on (.) I won't tell you again

Transcription key	
(.)	normal pause

Text A (continued)

Scenario 2: Jo is in a departmental meeting at work – 12.30pm. Lynn is Jo's boss.

L: so what kind of CPD training do you want this year Jo

J: erm well (2.0) I've not really thought about it

L: maybe something to help stretch and challenge the top grade students

J: erm (.) yes (.) that'd be good

L: ok (.) what about differentiation (.) what are you doing to ensure you differentiate your tasks as you've got lots of mixed ability groups this year

J: well (.) erm

Scenario 3: Jo has just returned to her car and a parking attendant is issuing her a ticket – 5.30pm.

PA: is this your car Madam

J: yes

PA: do you realise you were parked on a double yellow line

J: erm (.) well (.) erm (.) I'm so sorry (.) I just [popped]

PA: [I'm issuing] you with a fine (.) if you pay it within two weeks it'll cost fifty per cent less

Scenario 4: Jo is having dinner with a close friend, Helen – 8pm.

J: so (.) you'll never guess what happened to me earlier

H: what

J: I only went and got a bloody parking ticket (.) I only nipped across the road to grab some milk (.) I was gone for like (.) three minutes (.) max (.) then I get back and this bloody idiot in a yellow jacket's standing there staring at me and is all like (.) is this your car (.) God I could've cried (.) a hundred quid it is

H: no way (.) gutted man

Transcription key

(.)   normal pause

(2.0)   numbers in brackets indicate length of pause in seconds

[ ]   long brackets show simultaneous speech

Key term

Endearment: An affectionate term used to address someone without using the person's name.

Tip

When you see instances of simultaneous speech, it is important to gain an understanding of its use. For example, is it cooperative overlap to support the speaker or competitive interruption used to gain power in the exchange?

Activity 8

It is important to remember that the power balance can often shift within an exchange and can operate at a subtle level. For example, in Text A Scenario 3, it may seem that the parking attendant holds all the power, but Jo also has some power: notice that he adopts a concessionary approach to Jo, explaining that she can get a cheaper rate if she pays early. In the interaction with her son in Scenario 1, Jo uses a term of **endearment** to get her son on side (when she calls him 'sweetheart'), and this demonstrates her need to work hard to get him to do as she wants; she can't rely on any assumed power.

The sentence starters below sum up some of the broad AO3 points. Complete the sentences by adding:

- a quotation
- a linguistic analysis of this quotation
- further discussion and evaluation, linking back to relevant contextual factors.

For each interaction, make some notes on how the speakers attempt to assert and claim power.

1. In Scenario 1, Jo is clearly attempting to claim power over Seb (due to her role as his mother), when she uses the mitigated imperative 'come on Seb (.) it's time to get your coat on'. It is early in the morning and Jo is keen to leave the house. Because Seb isn't very cooperative about putting his coat on, Jo's language alters throughout the exchange _____

_____

_____

_____

_____

_____

_____

_____

2. In Scenario 2, which appears to be a fairly formal meeting between two work colleagues, Lynn seems to be in control of the conversation and she attempts to claim power due to her position as Jo's boss. Lynn does this through the use of _____

_____

_____

_____

_____

_____

_____

_____

3. In Scenario 3, Jo shows her shock at being reprimanded by the parking attendant, who is clearly claiming power through his position in this exchange. Jo appears anxious and shows deference towards the parking attendant through the use of _____

_____

_____

_____

_____

4. In Scenario 4, which is an informal spontaneous exchange with a close friend over dinner, Jo shows her disgust at receiving her parking ticket. She does this through the use of _____

_____

_____

_____

_____

_____

Structuring exam responses

So far you have examined the importance of contextual factors and have practised identifying and interpreting how language and context work together to create meanings and representations in spoken texts. You will now look at longer exam-style transcripts and practise your analysis skills, with particular focus on structuring your responses.

Tip

Remember that you are aiming to apply linguistic methods and terminology, identifying 'patterns and complexities' (Level 5 descriptor); you therefore need to be able to group together similar features that occur throughout the text. In the text on page 32, for example, you could group together the non-fluency features that are used throughout the text and discuss the impact these have on the text.

Activity 9

Carefully read the transcript in Text B which is a spontaneous exchange between two female friends, Amy and Sam. They are discussing Sam's sister. Analyse and annotate the transcript as you read; some annotations have been done for you, but you will need to add more detail yourself.

Identify the features listed below (as well as any other language features that you consider important here):

- an open question
- back-channel noises
- unvoiced pauses

- elision
- clippings
- fillers

- a tag question
- idiomatic expressions

Text B

The informal pronunciation of 'yer' reflects the casual nature of the exchange.

Amy: how yer doing Sam

Sam: not bad thanks

Amy: how's things with your sister at the mo

Sam: not good at the minute (.) she's broken up with Josh again

Amy: oh God (.) what's happened now

The use of open questions pass the floor to Sam; Sam responds and turn-taking is cooperative. The overlaps from Amy demonstrate her supporting her friend during this seemingly difficult time.

Sam: well she found out he was cheating on her with (.) you know Becky's cousin (2.0) she was in the year [below us at school]

Amy: [ah yeah I remember]

Sam: so (.) she came home one day and he just said (.) like (.) it's over

Amy: bloody hell

Sam: I know (.) she's absolutely gutted (.) [well beyond gutted (.)]

Amy: [I bet]

Sam: it's all over Facebook (.) she says she doesn't wanna go out or see anyone (.) so (.) it's been pretty difficult to be honest (.) I've been going over when I can (.) but

Amy: I can imagine (.) it must be really hard to know what to (.) are you ok

Sam: yeah suppose (.) mum and dad are pretty [cut up too cos]

Amy: [yeah they really liked him] didn't they

Sam uses a number of **declaratives** to explain to Amy the situation with her sister. Towards the end of the transcript, Sam begins to express some slightly negative attitudes towards her sister, for example, through the use of the idioms 'driving me a bit mad' and 'bit my head off'.

Sam: yep (.) he was part of the family really (.) we all thought they'd like (.) get married to be honest (.) it's a shock for everyone (3.0) my sister's driving me a bit mad though cos all she's doing is crying and not really being that nice to my parents (.) it's hard on them cos they just wanna help but she won't really let them (.) I took some food over for her the other day (.) trying to help (.) but she practically bit my head off

Transcription key

(.)	normal pause
(2.0)	numbers in brackets indicate length of pause in seconds
[]	long brackets show simultaneous speech

Roles – the two participants are clearly close friends; Amy knows about Sam's family and she asks questions about Sam's life. She is cooperative and listens to Sam, regularly back-channelling and offering conversational support to her friend.

Key term

Declarative: A clause or sentence that has a statement function.

An example Paper 1 spoken language question

Now you have developed an understanding of the requirements for this part of the exam, it is time to look at a typical Question 1 based on spoken data.

Tip

For Paper 1, Section A, remember to spend roughly 20 minutes reading and preparing both texts and noting down relevant contextual factors. Answer the who, where, when, and why questions. Once you feel you've got a good handle on the data, begin to annotate the text using appropriate and concise terminology, from a range of language levels.

> Analyse how the text uses language to create meanings and representations. **[25 marks]**

Introduction

You only have about 30 minutes to write your response, therefore it is important that your opening paragraph is clear and concise so you can move straight on to your analysis paragraphs. You need to show the examiner that you have a good overview of the data, so it is useful to briefly summarise some of the main contextual factors that affect the exchange as well as the ideas and attitudes expressed by the speakers. However, it is important that you don't simply reiterate the information that is already given to you on the exam paper.

Activity 10

Carefully read Text C opposite, which is a transcript of a husband and wife discussing their feelings about spiders. Answer the following questions.

1. List the contextual factors that may impact on the language used in this exchange.

_____

_____

2. What attitudes do Matt and Tess put forward about spiders?

_____

_____

_____

3. Write an introduction which contains an overview of the data (include the most salient aspects of context and attitudes).

_____

_____

_____

_____

Text C

Matt: So where did your fear of spiders come from

Tess: I dunno really (.) I think (.) my mum's always been scared of spiders so (.) maybe it's linked to that (.) hard to say

Matt: don't you think you can be a bit irrational at times (.) I mean (.) you even hate the ones that are [really]

Tess: [it's not] irrational at all (.) and some of them are massive anyway (.) I just hate the way they crawl (.) the ones with the long spindly legs are the worst (.) and (.) there's actually (.) poisonous [ones that]

Matt: [I know but] in this country you only get tiny ones (.) and they're harmless

Tess: well actually (.) what about that story the other week (.) in the news (.) where was it again (.) where they found the black widow spiders

Matt: oh about them being found in a warehouse (.) in Halesfield

Tess: yeah see (.) that's mega scary

Matt: Yeah [but]

Tess: [cos] they came over in the fruit

Matt: yeah but that's like (.) really rare

Tess: it does happen though (.) there were like five or six poisonous spiders (.) they just like opened the boxes of (.) erm (.) bananas was it (2.0) and saw these massive black widow spiders (.) scary or what (2.0) could've killed someone (.) it's a bloody good job (.) I wonder how they knew they were poisonous

Matt: dunno but they were definitely venomous (.) the exotic zoo's got them now (.) it was on the front page of the paper

Tess: I know (.) they can kill you with a single bite

Matt: yeah venomous ones can (.) but not normal house spiders (.) the worst they'd do is bite you but (.) you'd hardly notice it (.) it might itch a bit but (.) that's it (.) they run away from you most of the time

Tess: that's the worst (.) when they run really quick

Matt: it's bad luck to kill a spider anyway (.) that's what my Nan used to say

Tess: is it

Matt: yeah (2.0) but anyway (.) you do need to try and sort out this irrational fear (.) cos

Tess: it's a **pho**bia (.) I can't just **sort** it out

Matt: but you're gonna make the kids scared (.) I mean (.) Eve cries if she sees an ant

Tess: you can't blame me for that (.) I don't mind ants

Transcription key

(.)	normal pause
(1.0)	numbers in brackets indicate length of pause in seconds
bold	indicates a stressed syllable
[ ]	long brackets show simultaneous speech

Stretch

Record a series of your own conversations. Try and include a mixture of ages and cover both males and females. Transcribe them and think about the meanings that are being conveyed. How are topics, people and events being represented? Highlight the meanings and representations then annotate these sections using precise linguistic terms.

Analysis

Once you have written a short introductory paragraph, you need to get straight into your analysis paragraphs. However, before you write anything, it's important that you have a really good understanding of the meanings and representations and how these are expressed through language.

Here is a possible way to approach Questions 1 and 2:

1. Read the text for a quick overview. Outline relevant contextual factors affecting discourse choices.

2. Create a mind map of the contextual factors and representations. Think about how the text represents its subject matter. Consider different things that are represented in the texts – people, objects, companies, and so on – and ensure you have a firm grasp of *the way in which* they are represented, for example, the attitudes and ideas that are presented.

3. Read the texts again and highlight key sections from each text that illustrate the representations.

4. Once you have a clear understanding of context and meanings, carefully analyse the language use, always linking it to some aspect of context. Try and cover a range of language levels. Annotate the data using precise linguistic terminology.

5. Begin writing your answer.

Tip

Consider using electronic mind map makers such as Coggle (https://coggle. it/?lang=en-GB) to help organise your notes, or online quizzes such as Quizlet (https:// quizlet.com/en-gb) or Kahoot (https://kahoot. com/) to help test your knowledge. There are lots of pre-written quizzes or you can devise your own. You could also consider using apps to help with revision, for example, Brainscape allows you to make flashcards.

Activity 11

Do this exercise in 30 minutes. Follow steps 1–5 above and write up your response to the data in Text C on separate paper. Answer this exam question:

Analyse how **Text C** uses language to create meanings and representations.   **[25 marks]**

Activity 12

Once you have written up your response, use two different coloured highlighters to identify where you have carried out AO1 and AO3 work.

- Have you taken into account contextual factors and have you shown that you really understand what Tess and Matt's attitudes are? (AO3)

- How precise and wide-ranging are the linguistic descriptions you have used? Is your response carefully organised?

The texts that you are set for Paper 1 can be written, spoken or electronic in mode. In this section, we will look at effective ways to revise the analysis of this last mode: electronic or computer-mediated communication (CMC).

Activity 1

Gather a set of your own data and that of family and friends to help you revise. Find some or all of the following:

- social media posts and comments

- online news stories with posts and comments

- posts on message boards

- blog posts

- emails.

Use your data to test out some of the analytical approaches outlined throughout this chapter.

The **scope** of CMC grows all the time and you could be set any form of this to analyse. While the range of possible texts is huge, the same principles of analysis that you have been revising in the previous chapters still apply. All texts – whether they are written, spoken or electronic – are created by text producers to create meanings, and the language of these texts will demonstrate choices that have been made. But remember, all texts are produced making use of the *affordances* of a given mode and within the *limitations* of it too.

> **Key term**
>
> **Scope:** How far a study extends, how much is covered.

Activity 2

1. Remind yourself of what these terms mean.

Affordances: _____

Limitations: _____

2. Copy and complete the table on page 40 with at least two affordances and one limitation for each of the forms of computer-mediated or electronic communication listed, compared to what a straightforward written text would be capable of offering. An example has been provided.

Technology	Affordance	Limitation
Twitter	• Allows you to hold short, interactive 'conversations' with multiple users almost instantly • You can embed links which might be photos, gifs, memes	• Limited number of characters per tweet (was 140 but now 280)
Facebook		
Snapchat		
Email		
Text message		
Online message board/ discussion forum		

When communicating using these forms of technology, text producers can interact in ways that share some aspects with spoken language, making use of interactional features and collaborating to create meanings together.

Activity 3

Read the following tweets and make a note of the ways in which these use some of the interactional features of spoken language.

a. Is it just me or is this time of year the worst for toddlers? So moody and tantrum-prone!
♡ 5 💬 2

b. Well…I did it! I've only gone and handed in my notice. Now for stage 2 of my life!!!

c. Well done you ☺ Soooo pleased

d. Yeah right, that was *really* necessary

e. What do you mean?

f. Err, the way he stamped on his leg after going through him in the tackle?

g. *Does Wenger voice* I didn't see anything

As well as being interactive, CMC can be multimodal, that is, it can make use of different modes of communication such as: written text, audio, video and animated images.

Representing your identity online

When analysing CMC texts, you can focus on the ways in which text producers represent their subject matter, but you can also explore how they represent and position themselves through a range of language choices and interactions. For example, you could look at usernames, profile pictures and the use of 'like' or 'favourite' responses.

All texts – written, spoken and CMC – exist within a context. Part of the context for CMC texts might be their online existence. For example, an article in a newspaper that appears online will exist in a different context from that of the physical edition.

Activity 4

Look at the annotations around Text A below and add your own to the areas indicated.

Text A

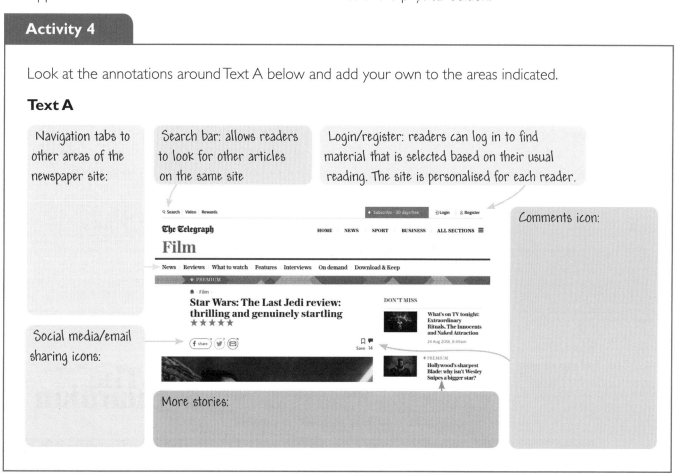

Navigation tabs to other areas of the newspaper site:

Search bar: allows readers to look for other articles on the same site

Login/register: readers can log in to find material that is selected based on their usual reading. The site is personalised for each reader.

Comments icon:

Social media/email sharing icons:

More stories:

Activity 5

In the example that follows, a student has started to analyse Text B on pages 42–43. After the opening section, there is a short commentary by the examiner, highlighting why this is a good start and suggesting a few areas of improvement.

Read the student's analysis and the examiner commentary. What do you think this student is doing well for both AO1 and AO3 and where could they improve? On separate paper, rewrite the student's analysis and improve it, taking into account the examiner's comments. Add another three or four short paragraphs to focus on other areas of meaning and representation in the text.

Student response:

In this online text commentary the text producers (Geoff Lemon and Rod Smyth of *The Guardian* website) are describing the events of the cricket match as they take place. Because this is an online commentary using text rather than video, they have to convey the events in a way that captures the excitement of the match and both inform and entertain the audience, who will be following this on a phone or PC, probably somewhere a long way from Australia where it is taking place.

The structure of the text is interesting because it begins at the top with the most recent events in the match and is organised chronologically where the older posts are nearer the bottom of the page. This means that for the reader, the most recent action is given prominence and made more obvious.

Because the commentary is using text, the writing makes use of the affordances of the written mode such as the bold font for the verb 'dropped' in the line 'Malan is **dropped** off the first delivery...'. If this had been spoken, the verb might have been emphasised with stress to show how significant a moment this was, but here it is highlighted by the font. On the other hand, one of the limitations of the written mode for a text like this which is typed on a keyboard as the action is happening, and not edited by someone else, is that typos and errors can creep in. This can be seen in the post where the writer says 'Smith canh't get through his over...'.

Examiner commentary:

This is a good start and there is plenty to credit in this analysis. The student starts by looking at what is being described here (the cricket match) and then links this to the mode of the text. He moves on to consider discourse structure and context, before focusing on some language detail that is used to represent actions in the game. He links it to mode again and quotes some examples to illustrate.

Where it could be improved is perhaps to start by giving a better picture of what is happening in the match, a bit more focus on the events themselves and more sense of the whole text. (What else is there on the page apart from the running commentary?) It might also be interesting to think about the audience who would have to know quite a lot of field-specific lexis to understand this commentary and the opinions and viewpoints that are being offered on the action.

Text B

4m ago
DAVID MALAN MAKES HIS FIRST TEST CENTURY!!

1h ago
AUSTRALIA REVIEW! England 217 - 4 (Malan not out)

3h ago
Tea

4h ago
WICKET! Stoneman c Paine b Starc 56 (England 131-4)

4h ago
WICKET! Root c Paine b Cummins 20

4h ago
Dropped!

5h ago
Half century! Stoneman 52 from 82 balls

15m ago
09:34

82nd over: England 276-4 (Malan 93, Bairstow 63) Malan is **dropped** off the first delivery with the second new ball! He edged a drive at Starc towards third slip, where Bancroft moved too far across to his right and felt the ball whoosh between his arms. It's a wonderful first over back from Starc. Bairstow is beaten, edges along the floor to the boundary and finally digs out a yorker. This should be a tremendous half-hour.

22m ago
09:27

81st over: England 271-4 (Malan 92, Bairstow 59) Marsh is continuing with the old ball, a surprising decision as the one is available. When he drifs onto the pads, Bairstow flicks easily for four and probably ensures this will be Marsh's final over of the day.

26m ago
09:24

80th over: England 267-4 (Malan 92, Bairstow 55) Smith canh't get through his over quickly enough. He bowls six dot balls to Mailan, who thus stays on 92. It's time for the **second new ball**.

29m ago
09:20

79th over: England 267-4 (Malan 92, Bairstow 55) Starc and Hazlewood are preparing for one last crack with the second new ball. Marsh bowls a maiden to the watchul Bairstow.

33m ago
09:17

78th over: England 267-4 (Malan 92, Bairstow 55) Malan late cuts Smith four three to move into the nineties. That drum-and-bass track you can hear is his heartbeat. He's eight runs away from a Test century. A Test *century*. A *Test* century.

36m ago
09:14

77th over: England 262-4 (Malan 89, Bairstow 53) Marsh (4-0-18-0) switches ends and is glided sweetly for four by Bairstow. That takes him to a superb **fifty**, an innings of impressive authority. Two balls later he does well to dig out a beautiful yorker from Marsh.

     Updated at 9.15am GMT

40m ago
09:10

76th over: England 257-4 (Malan 89, Bairstow 48) Steve Smith replaces Mitchell Marsh and tempts Malan into chasing a very wide delivery beats the bat. Don't do it Dawid!

"Perth Tests are the only ideal ones in Oregon - starts after the workday and ends at a reasonable time to sleep 2-30 ish," says Zaph Mann. "But I sense you are in a sleep limbo, so calm is your commentary, or are you just hoping that massive placation ensures this duo continue as long as possible?"

When you have Ashes insomnia you've never really asleep ... and you're never really awake.

Most of what you have covered so far has been about focusing on single texts. In this section, you will look in more detail at what to do for Question 3 in Paper 1, Section A, and how to explore similarities and differences between texts.

A key part of doing well in Section A is using your time sensibly, making plenty of notes and coming up with a plan before you start writing. As you read and think about Texts A and B for Questions 1 and 2, you can also make some useful notes for Question 3.

As you have seen in the chapters on written, spoken and multimodal texts, context is important to understanding and interpreting meanings. Context is also important for approaching Question 3 where you are asked to explore the similarities and differences between the two texts.

The two texts are always on the same topic or theme, so that is one initial point of similarity to look at. However, while the texts are on the same topic, they will handle it differently, representing it in different ways, offering varying perspectives and using language in ways affected by many contextual factors. In Question 3 your job is to explore those similarities and differences.

One way to organise your answer is to think about how each of the following varies from text to text:

- audience
- mode
- time

- purpose
- genre
- place.

These can then be used as a structure for your answer, alongside your discussion of the subject matter and the language being used.

Obviously, as you are discussing Text A and Text B again, you will find that you need to refer to examples and points of interest that you might have already raised in your answers to Questions 1 and 2. This is not a problem. You can repeat some points but you will need to remember that you are being assessed using AO4, so you will need to find *connections* to discuss. You also need to remember that your points must be evidenced with clear examples from the texts and that you must discuss the language used in detail.

The examples that follow refer to texts you have already looked at in the chapters *Paper 1, Section A: Analysing written texts*; *Paper 1, Section A: Analysing spoken texts*; and *Paper 1, Section A: Computer-mediated communication*. This chapter provides you with a further text to go alongside each of them. These will then form pairs of texts that are similar to those on Paper 1 of the A level exam.

Exam-style questions

Activity 1

The three tasks that follow use some of the texts you have already looked at in the previous chapters, then provide you with a new text on the same topic to go alongside them. For each pair of texts (and the Stretch texts at the end of the chapter) you can use the following question format and write your own plan, notes and timed response on separate paper.

1. Analyse how the first text uses language to create meanings and representations.   **[25 marks]**

2. Analyse how the second text uses language to create meanings and representations.   **[25 marks]**

3. Explore the similarities and differences in the ways that the first text and the second text use language.   **[20 marks]**

Paired text analysis task 1

Refer back to Text C on page 37, the transcript in which Matt and Tess discuss spiders.

Text 1 below is taken from the *Singleton Argus* (New South Wales), published on Saturday 6 March 1897. As part of the Commonwealth, Australian newspapers often published news from other English-speaking countries.

Text 1

British & foreign news

The following extracts are taken from files by the English mail: –

Among the spiders

James Payn, a native of Liverpool, is now in hospital in Portland (Oregon), recovering from an attack of insanity, the result of a strange incident. Last October he started on his way across the Continent, and visited various cities. At one railway station he entered a car loaded with bananas, and, having eaten a few, fell asleep. When he awoke the door was sealed, and the train was in motion. Payn thought it would soon stop, and went to sleep, but was awakened by something crawling over his face. He struck a match, and discovered numerous tarantulas, one of which as he looked up fell upon his forehead, causing him to fall fainting. Upon recovering, he tried the door, but was unable to open it. The number of tarantulas steadily increased as they made their way out of the bunches of bananas, and all that day and night Payn leaned against the side of the car afraid to move, and with the spiders everywhere, and even crawling over him. He fainted again, and when he recovered consciousness he found himself in a cot in the hospital in Portland. It seems that when the car was opened upon reaching its destination Payn was found in its back. A mark on the forehead showed where he had been bitten.

Paired text analysis task 2

Refer back to Text B on pages 42–43, the online cricket commentary.

Text 2 below is taken from the *Australian Women's Weekly* of 1 December 1934.

Text 2

ENGLAND'S *girl* CRICKETERS *are* GOOD SPORTS

'Put Larwood On' Was Cry

From Our Perth Representative

MISS BETTY ARCHDALE, captain of the English team, who so successfully led her team to victory in the match England versus Western Australia.

The English women's cricket team have played their first match in Australia and incidentally created many records. A record crowd was present on the opening day, a good-tempered humorous crowd of nearly four thousand who watched with interest as the women wielded their bats and sent the ball scurrying to the boundaries.

Miss M. Hide must be credited with being the first woman cricketer to score a century in international cricket.

ON the other hand the English cricketers had their first introduction to the Australian barracker. Good naturedly they soon had names for the players, and implored the captain (Miss Archdale) to 'Put Larwood on' – 'Larwood' being the name given to Miss Taylor, the fast bowler of the side.

Miss Taylor later said she had no desire to emulate her male model and raise a howl from the hill, but she took the barracking she received with good grace.

How They Dress

ALREADY their cricket uniform has created interest. They played in the match wearing divided skirts, and shirts made of linen which open at the neck, and have short sleeves. Their hats are of a light fabric, with tropical gauze lining. They wear thick white stockings, and spiked shoes are favored for batting and in the field occasionally. They have rubber soled shoes, but are doubtful if these will be utilised in the very hot weather. Their blazers are of white with the mono-gram W.C.A.T.T., which stand for Women's Cricket Association Touring Team.

In an interview with Miss Betty Archdale, who captained the English team, she said, 'No we do not play with men, or in any way strive to emulate them. I admit the men have helped us wonderfully, lending us their grounds, giving us tuition, and assisting us in every possible way.'

IN reference to a remark on the winning of the Ashes, Miss Archdale immediately replied, 'Please tell Australia we are not here to play for any Ashes, but merely to play Test cricket. It is very much against the principle of the English Women's Cricket Association to play for trophies or anything of that sort. Please tell the people we are here to play England versus Australia cricket, and would much rather the term Ashes was not used.' With that, Miss Green, the manager, with a twinkle in her eye said, 'The only likely ashes will be our team in Brisbane if the climate is any hotter than it is today in Perth.' When told it was a mild summer's day, the whole team drew out their hand-kerchiefs, mopped their brows, and murmured. 'Oh, dear.' This action at once stamped the English team as great humorists, and this trace of humor will undoubtedly make them popular with the Australians. The girls are of a fine athletic type, extremely pleasant, quick to see a joke, and are very team-minded.

MEMBERS of the English women's cricket team, who participated in the match played at Perth. Back Row from Left: M. MacLagan, M. Child, J. Patridge, B. Archdale (captain), J. Liebert, M. Richards, M. Taylor. Front Row: G. Morgan, H. Green, M. Spear, M. Burleston, E. Snowball, and D. Turner. M. Hide, who made a century in her first innings in Australia, and C. Valentine were absent when this photograph was taken.

Transcription key

(.)	normal pause
bold	indicate a stressed syllable
[ ]	long brackets show simultaneous speech

Paired text analysis task 3

Refer back to Text F on pages 21–22, the 1960 review of the film *Psycho*.

Text 3 below is a transcript of two friends, Anton and Clare, discussing films.

Text 3

Clare: you've always been into horror films really haven't you (.) like Friday the thirteenth and that

Anton: yeah (.) I tell you what freaked me out the most was that **It** (.) you know the Stephen King (.) the clown

Clare: oh yeah

Anton: it's just a bit messed up (.) the clown (.) and dagger

Clare: yeah

Anton: the thing that's always frightened me about horror is like (.) the suspense of it (.) like (.) it's not the blood or the actual horror (.) it's the unknown (.) it's almost like the anticipation leading up to an event rather than the event itself

Clare: yeah it's like that in The Shining isn't it (.) who was that again

Anton: Jack Nicholas

Clare: Jack Nichol**son**

Anton: yeah that's it (.) it was the psychological aspect of it wasn't it (.) rather than the [actual]

Clare: [yeah (.)] there's that famous line isn't there that everyone talks about

Anton: here's Johnny

Clare: yeah everyone's heard of that

Anton: yeah it's like a lot of those (.) there was all the Scream films weren't there (.) you know (.) and then there was like (.) Final Destination (.) and those kind of films (.) they were like gore-fests

Clare: yeah (.) I Know What You Did Last Summer

Anton: loads of blood (.) but they weren't **that** scary (.) it was more like Nightmare on Elm Street

Clare: was that one of the first horror films

Anton: well (.) the first horror films were from the 60s (.) the Hammer ones (.) Christopher Lee as Dracula (.) they were a bit camp to be honest (.)

Stretch

You can practise more text analysis for Paper 1 by using two other texts from earlier in the book and the question format given to you on page 45.

Use Text E on page 21 (the 1933 car advert) and find a more recent advert for a car, either from a brochure or from a car dealership website.

Use Text G on page 23 (the account of the Peterloo Massacre) and find a more recent account of a political demonstration or instance of public disorder from a newspaper website.

One of the two areas on which you will be set a question is children's spoken language. To answer these questions effectively, you will need to consider the idea in the question and the data that has been provided to go with it. This will require a balanced and integrated approach that allows you to look at concepts and debates around how children acquire language, as well as draw on a detailed discussion and understanding of examples (from the data provided and from your own study).

In this chapter you will have the chance to revise both concepts and data analysis skills before looking at exam-style questions and considering how to plan and write answers effectively.

Knowledge about children's early language

Activity 1

How does children's language develop? You will have studied a range of different developments across a range of different levels (for example, their vocabulary, syntax, the sounds they make). Copy and complete the table below, noting down two or three ideas per language level. Some prompts have been offered to get you started.

Language level	Questions about development
Lexis	What are children's most common early words? What trends are there in children's vocabulary development?
Semantics	What errors do children often make with word meanings? Do children understand more about what words mean than they can produce in their own language?
Phonology	What sounds come first for most children? What kinds of errors do children make in sound production?
Syntax	What stages do children go through? What kinds of words do children often combine?
Morphology	Which word endings do children use and why are they significant? Which common morphology errors have you studied?
Pragmatics	How do areas such as **politeness** and **inference** develop as children get older? How do children behave in conversations with others as they develop?

Key terms

Inference: Using assumed knowledge in order to determine meaning.

Politeness: An aspect of pragmatics that refers to the cultural rules of a community and regulates how social relationships are negotiated. Everyday use of the term 'polite' tends to be associated with surface aspects such as table manners and saying 'please' and 'thank you'. These aspects are connected with the academic concept but it goes much deeper than this, including all aspects of cultural rules about appropriate language use in social engagements.

You will probably have mentioned things like the different words and sounds children might use and the length of what they say compared to adult speech, but it is also worth thinking about the *functions* of language if you haven't already. As we grow older, we have to put language to use in a much more varied range of contexts and we need to be flexible and adapt how we use language.

Activity 2

When children first start using language, they have quite a limited **repertoire**. M.A.K. Halliday suggested in his taxonomy that children use the following functions. Complete the table below giving a definition and example for each.

Function	Definition and example
Instrumental	
Regulatory	
Interactional	
Personal	
Heuristic	
Imaginative	
Representational	

Children's language is less grammatically developed at early ages than that of adults. One of the ways in which child language researchers have categorised children's language is into stages which are related to the complexity of children's utterances, in terms of the nature of the sounds they make and the number of words they use.

Activity 3

Look at the stages below and put them in the right order, with a short definition next to each and an example of the kind of utterance a child might make at that stage.

Stage	Order (1–8)	Definition and examples
Post-telegraphic		
Telegraphic		
Holophrastic/ one word		
Two word		

Stage	Order (1–8)	Definition and examples
Vegetative		
Babbling		
Cooing		
Proto-word		

Analysing children's early language

It is important to have plenty of examples of children's language to refer to in your answers so that you can illustrate how children are using language (and how it is used towards them). Some of the examples can come from the data you are given in the question itself, but you can also draw on your own notes and research. It is important to be able to describe linguistically what is happening in the data.

Activity 4

Look at the examples of language in Table A and produce a linguistic description of what the child is doing. Concentrate not just on errors but what the child is getting right (in terms of how close it is to adult speech). One example has been completed for you. Copy and complete the rest of the table.

Table A

Utterance	Linguistic description
'I walking daddy'	The child is using a telegraphic utterance to describe to her dad what she is doing. Classifying this with Halliday's taxonomy, she is using a representational function because she is describing an action she is carrying out. She is using a verb in the progressive **aspect** (walking) but the utterance is telegraphic because she has omitted the **auxiliary verb** *am*.
'I hungry'	
'Mummy putted them in the basket'	
'I not like that juice'	
'We saw the ducks in the pond'	

Key terms

Aspect: The way in which certain grammatical markings on verb forms indicate whether an action or state is ongoing. For example, the 'ing' form in 'looking' suggests continuous action: the 'ing' ending is called a 'progressive'.

Auxiliary verb: A verb that helps other verbs. Auxiliary verbs include 'be', 'do' and 'have'.

Holophrastic: Holophrase means 'whole phrase' and, as it suggests, refers to the stage of language acquisition where whole phrases can be expressed via a single word. Also called the one-word stage.

Post-telegraphic: A developmental stage that goes beyond children's use of abbreviated speech.

Repertoire: The range of language forms or styles used by a speaker.

The examples in Table A are largely to do with the syntax of children's early language (that is, the ways in which they put words together into grammatical structures to create meanings), but it is also useful to look at their phonological and semantic development.

Table B in Activity 5 gives you examples of utterances children have made which don't sound exactly like the adult version. The **phonemic alphabet** has been used to describe these sounds (see below).

Activity 5

For each of the examples of language in Table B, fill in the phonological process the child has used. One example has been completed for you and other terms have been listed at the end for you to choose from.

Table B

Child says	Phonological process
'gog' when describing a dog	Assimilation (child has assimilated the /g/ sound in 'dog'.)
'doggie'	
'Mummy is on puter' when saying 'computer'	
'I got my dink' – waving cup with drink in	
'I putting my coa on' when putting coat on	
'Dese my sweeties' – pointing at packet of sweets	

deletion   consonant cluster reduction

addition   deletion of unstressed syllable   substitution

Activity 6

1. Children's understanding and use of words is another key element of early language development. Remind yourself of two important aspects of this by revising the ideas of language production and language comprehension. What is the difference? Write a short explanation for each in the spaces below.

Language production: _____

_____

_____

Language comprehension: _____

_____

_____

2. Another area you can revise to help you to prepare for the exam is children's early lexical and semantic development. Gather examples of children's early words from your class notes, textbook and own research. Categorise these examples by the things they refer to (the topics or fields) and the grammatical categories they belong to (word classes such as nouns, verbs and adjectives). Look too at any *extension* errors children make.

Remind yourself of the different kinds of extension and write a short explanation with examples for each.

Categorical overextension: _____

_____

_____

Analogical overextension: _____

_____

_____

Predicate statement/mismatch: _____

_____

_____

Underextension: _____

_____

_____

Key terms

Behaviourism / Behaviourist: Within studies of language acquisition, a notion of learned behaviour as a set of responses to stimuli.

Child-Directed Speech (CDS): The speech that parents and caregivers use to children.

Cognitive: Thinking processes in the brain.

Construction: In language acquisition, constructions are ready-made chunks of language that can be used productively to express many ideas. This model is also called a usage-based approach.

Nativist / Nativism: A belief that language acquisition relies on an inbuilt capacity for language in humans.

Pivot schema: The use by children of certain key words as a 'pivot' to generate many utterances.

Revising the key theories and research

One of the key elements of answering the question on children's spoken language development effectively is to engage with the view that you are asked to evaluate. The view will generally relate to different ideas and arguments about how and why children's language develops. As you will have studied, there are competing explanations for language development and different schools of thought about how it happens.

Activity 7

Remind yourself what is meant by the terms below in relation to language development and write a short definition for each.

Nature: _____

_____

_____

Nurture: _____

_____

_____

In the past, the debate has often been polarised into a 'nature versus nurture' argument, but increasingly, linguists and psychologists acknowledge the important role of both elements. In fact, the linguist Rebecca Woods says this about the debate: 'It's not a question of nature versus nurture; it's more a question of the nature of the nature and the nature of the nurture'.

Activity 8

You will have studied a range of different theories related to children's language development as part of your course and it is important to have a clear idea about their main arguments and how to evaluate what they have said.

Match the theorists listed below to the theory.

Theorist	Theory
Noam Chomsky	**Behaviourist** theory and operant conditioning
B.F. Skinner	Social interaction theory and the role of **Child-Directed Speech (CDS)**
Lev Vygotsky	**Nativist** / generativist theory and universal grammar
Jean Piaget	Usage-based theory and the importance of '**constructions**'
Jerome Bruner	**Cognitive** theory
Michael Tomasello	Cognitive theory and the importance of interaction and play

Make sure you have clear notes on each of the thinkers listed in Activity 8 and that you understand what they have argued around language development. For example, make sure you have notes on the features of CDS and the evidence for and against nativist and behaviourist theories. It is also important to reference the work of language researchers, so check the following names and ideas in your textbook to make sure you have covered a range of areas: Jean Berko-Gleason's wug-test, George Braine's **pivot schema**, Deb Roy's speechome project.

Integrating the data and ideas

In the exam you are given a view to evaluate and data to draw upon. The balance of marks is equal for AO1 and AO2, so it is important to strike a similar balance in what you write, engaging with and evaluating the view that is being put forward, while using – and linguistically describing – the language children produce and/or that is used towards them. The following task offers some ways into this before you move on to look at some exam-style questions.

Activity 9

The table below shows analysis of an extract of conversation between a child and an adult. On a separate piece of paper create a similar table to analyse the list of utterances given on page 56. Look at each example and try and use linguistic terms to analyse the language used. Then try and relate the language use (of child and parent, if relevant) to theories of child **language acquisition**.

Example	Linguistic analysis	What theoretical concept could support this use of language?
Mum: Get ready, I'm going to throw the ball Child: me catched it	Here, the child is using an **object** pronoun in the **subject position** – a common grammatical error. The child is also demonstrating the use of a **virtuous error** in the form of overgeneralisation. The child is attempting to form the past tense of the dynamic verb 'catch' but because this verb is irregular, the child **overgeneralises** using the past tense '-ed'.	This example would support the theory of **innateness**. The child is clearly using a rule (add the '-ed' **inflection** to form a past tense verb) but unfortunately, because this verb is irregular, it doesn't follow this usual pattern. The over-application of these kinds of rules supports innateness and nature. It rejects nurture theories as clearly the child hasn't imitated this utterance.

Stretch

There are many other studies and individual pieces of research that could be relevant. These resources are worth looking at in more detail:

Paul Ibbotson's chapter 'Child Language Acquisition' in D. Clayton (ed.), *Language: a student handbook* (2nd edition) (London: English and Media Centre, 2018)

Matthew Saxton, *Child Language Acquisition and Development* (2nd edition) (London: Sage, 2017)

Key terms

Inflection: A morpheme on the end of a word to indicate a grammatical relationship or category. For example, many nouns in English add an 's' to indicate plurality.

Innate: Something inbuilt, already in place.

Language acquisition: The development of language within an individual.

Object: The thing or person on the receiving end of the action of the verb.

Overgeneralisation: Applying a rule and assuming that every example follows the same system, without realising that there are exceptions.

Subject position: The perspective taken on a topic, where some aspects are foregrounded and emphasised while others are downplayed.

Virtuous error: A mistake that has an underlying logic, showing that learning has taken place.

Examples
Dad: what's this one called
Child: issa tiger
Dad: nearly (.) it's a lion
[while looking at a picture book together]
Can you untighten this [when asking her mother to loosen her hair band]
It's spicy [when eating a fizzy sweet]
Child: Can I have a weetie
Mum: What do you say when you want a sweetie
Child: **Please** can I have a weetie
I'm more gooder than Seb [Seb is her brother]
My peel's coming off [when noticing a small graze on her knee]
Have you sawn it [when asking her mother if she has seen a picture she drew]

Stretch

Look at the examples again in Activity 9 and try and identify how you could group them together to show your understanding of patterns and complexities. For example, some utterances may contain grammatical errors, while others may contain semantic errors, phonological errors and so on.

Write a paragraph of analysis, grouping together the similar kinds of errors. Ensure you use the appropriate linguistic terminology and bring in relevant theory.

Dealing with exam questions

The next activity gives you the chance to plan and write an answer to an exam-style question. Questions in Section B always present you with an idea to evaluate and one or two data sets to analyse. This activity also gives you the beginning of a student response to the exam question.

Activity 10

Try to tackle this question in the same amount of time you would have in the exam: for Section B this is 10 minutes for reading/annotation and 40 minutes for writing.

'Children's linguistic development is the result of an innate capacity to learn language'.

Referring to **Data Set 1** and **Data Set 2** in detail, and to relevant ideas from language study, evaluate this view of children's language development.

[30 marks]

a. Carefully read the exam-style question on page 56 and identify the key words. Identify the different sides of the debate.

b. Read Data Sets 1 and 2 and annotate them. Decide which parts of the data you will use and which theories, studies and research will help you to answer the question and form an argument. What different angles could you take here? On separate paper, write a plan for your response.

c. Write your response on separate paper, ensuring you tackle the debate in the question while analysing the data (using linguistic terminology) and drawing in relevant concepts and research.

Transcription key

(.)	normal pause
(2.0)	numbers in brackets indicate length of pause in seconds
[looks at mother]	square brackets indicate paralinguistic features
::	elongated sound
/pɪswʊmən/	indicates phonemic symbols have been used

Data Set 1 and Data Set 2 are transcripts of Jess (three years old) with her mother. In Data Set 1 they are making a jigsaw. In Data Set 2 they are looking at picture cards together.

Data Set 1

Mum: where does this one go

Jess: I not know

Mum: you do

Jess: where

Mum: erm (.) where they go

Jess: what you do like that

Mum: where does this one go (.) where does this one go Jessie

Jess: it go in middle

Mum: in the middle

Jess: yeah

Mum: where's the nurse (.) where's that one

Jess: what

Mum: what about that one (.) where's the nurse one

Transcription key

(.)	normal pause
(2.0)	numbers in brackets indicate length of pause in seconds
bold	indicates a stressed syllable
[ ]	long brackets show simultaneous speech
[looks at mother]	square brackets indicate paralinguistic features
::	elongated sound

Jess: I not know

Mum: where does that one go (.) does it go there [Jess shakes her head] it is (.) look (.) there it is

Jess: no:: (.) I put em in the middle (.) I do em

Mum: shall we do their middles now (.) their tummies

Jess: yeah

Mum: where does that one go

Jess: look he got em there (.) got /pɪswʊmən/* (.) put them middle up there (.)

Mum: you going to put them together

Jess: yeah (.) no (.) them not go there

Mum: can you see where he goes (.) is that the clown

Jess: yeah (.) see which one tis (.) I get head together

Mum: what are you doing

Jess: heads together

Mum: putting their heads together (.) get their heads together

Jess: you put heads together (.) put their heads together

*policewoman

Data Set 2

Mum: Jess (.) [pointing to a picture] what's that one

Jess: duck quack quack

Mum: [pointing to picture] what noise does a horsey make

Jess: neigh

Mum: what does a busy bee do

Jess: bee:: [mother points to picture] zebra (.) tiger

Mum: what do tigers do

Jess: roar

Mum: have you ever seen a tiger [Jess shakes her head] no (.) what about when we went to the zoo (1.0) what's that

Jess: a goose (.) egg (.) a lion (.) a rainbow Pooh Bear (.) that's Pooh Bear

Mum: what's that

Jess: a ball (.) look got it over (.) a ball that's it over (.) that's the end

Mum: ooh [points to picture]

Jess: apple

Mum: where do you have apples

Jess: nursery

Mum: what else do you have at nursery

Jess: I not have no eating

Mum: oranges (.) bananas

Jess: nanas

Mum: where's daddy today

Jess: work

Mum: whose car did he take

Jess: mummy's

Mum: what's that [points to picture]

Jess: umbrella

Mum: and what do we use an umbrella for

Jess: rain

Mum: when it's rainy (.) what's that [points to picture]

Jess: gloo

Mum: eh

Jess: gloo

Mum: what is it

Jess: gloo

Mum: igloo (.) and what lives in igloos

Jess: penguins (.)

Mum: what's that [points to picture]

Jess: orange

Mum: right (.) and what colour is a banana

Jess: red

Mum: no (.) what else is yellow (2.0) what colour is an er apple

Jess: green

Transcription key

(.)	normal pause
(2.0)	numbers in brackets indicate length of pause in seconds
[points]	square brackets indicate paralinguistic features
bold	indicates a stressed syllable
[ ]	long brackets show simultaneous speech
::	elongated sound
/piswʊmən/	indicates phonemic symbols have been used

Mum: [starts singing] the wheels on the bus go

Jess: round and round all day long (.) the horn on the bus goes beep beep beep (.) beep beep beep (.) beep beep beep (.) horn on the bus goes beep beep beep (.) all day long

Mum: the babies on the bus go

Jess: cry cry cry (.) cry cry cry (.) the babies on the bus go cry cry cry (.) all day long

Mum: what about twinkle twinkle little star

Jess: no:: (.) want chock chock

Mum: twinkle twinkle

Jess: I want /tʃɒkət/*

Mum: tell you what (.) we'll sing twinkle twinkle little star then see what we can find (.) okay (.) ready

*chocolate

Activity 11

Here is a second exam-style question for you to work on using two more data sets. Use the same planning approach as set out in Activity 10.

> 'The acquisition of language depends primarily on children's interaction with the people and things around them'.
>
> Referring to **Data Set 3** and **Data Set 4** in detail, and to relevant ideas from language study, evaluate this view of children's language development.   **[30 marks]**

Data Set 3

This is a transcript between Seb (six years old) and his mother. It is bedtime and Seb is reading a Biff and Chip book to his mother.

Mother: no we're on this one look [points to the page] William looked in the hall **he's**

Seb: **he's** the

Mother: no no no look we're not on that one we're on here [points to a word on the page] **he's hid**den

Seb: (4.0) he's (.) hidden (.) the (.) egg (.) in (.) her

Mother: in **here** (2.0) he's hidden the egg in here (.) and what does that exclamation mark mean (.) at the end [uses rising intonation]

Seb: **he's hidden the heg* in here** [slow, deliberate speech with all syllables emphasised]

Mother: good

Seb: she (.) said (.) the (.) man (.) ssstarted (.) to (.) run (.) but (.) Biff trrrripped up (.) hip

Mother: tripped him

Seb: up (.) **crash crash** [throws arms in air excitedly]

Mother: so why did erm why did (.) Seb just look at that (.) tell me (.) why did (.) the man start to run

Seb: because he stole an egg and he wanted to run away

Mother: why did he steal the egg

Seb: cos erm he erm (.) cos he stole the egg and he wanted to run away cos they were trying to catch the egg off him

Mother: I don't (.) erm where did he get the egg from

Seb: he got the egg from the Golden Eagle's nest

Mother: ahhh ok (.) go on then read the next page (.) do your best reading

Seb: Max (.) took (.) the (.) egg (.) and (.) /wə/ (.) /rə/ (.) /ae/ (.) /pə/ (.) /edə/ (.) wapped

Mother: **wrapped**

Seb: wrapped (.) it (.) in (.) his (.) cash (.) cash

Mother: no start from (.) what's the first letter

Seb: /dʒ/ (.) /dʒ/

Mother: yeah

Seb: /dʒ/ (.) /dʒæk/ (.) /et/ too

Mother: jacket

Seb: **jack**et

Mother: yeah

Seb: Max (.) took (.) the (.) egg and wrapped it in his jacket to keep it warm there ⌈Wil ⌉

Mother: ⌊then⌋

Seb: then (.) Wilma (.) blew (.) the (.) horn (.) **boom** (.) **boom** (.) **boom**

Mother: **good** (.) can you remember that egg we had outside our house

*egg

Transcription key

(.)	normal pause
(2.0)	numbers in brackets indicate length of pause in seconds
[points]	square brackets indicate paralinguistic features
bold	indicates a stressed syllable
[ ]	long brackets show simultaneous speech

Seb: yeah

Mother: what did you do with it

Seb: I wrapped it in a glove

Mother: yeah

Seb: that was a good idea

Mother: it was (.) you basically did the same as what Max has done in this story didn't you

Data Set 4

This is a transcript between Ruby (two years and nine months) and her father. They are looking at a book called *Tales From Acorn Wood* together.

D   here we go (.)
R   dere
D   what shall we read
R   [indecipherable] da pig
D   which one (.) the pig one
R   yeah
D   OK what have we got (1.0) let's find the pig [turns pages] what does it say
R   pig
D   'let's play'…
R   hide and pig
D   'hide and seek,' says hen (.) 'Yes,' says pig 'I'll count to'…
R   ten (1.0) one (.) two (.) three (.) eight
D   [laughs] one (.) two (.) three (1.0) [four] (.)
R   [four]
D   five
R   six
D   seven (.) eight (.) nine (1.0)
R   [ten]
D   [ten] well done (1.0) 'Now it's time for pig to seek (.) can you see a yellow [beak]
R   [beak]
D   where's the beak (.) can you see one
R   [is looking away from book and slaps hand on page] dere
D   oh
R   [points at another picture] dere
D   blackbird (.) OK what's next (1.0) who's that
R   piggy
D   who's that (2.0)
R   what's that
D   blackbird
R   blackbird

One of the questions in Paper 1, Section B will be on children's written language development but, as you have seen in the work for Paper 1, Section A, written language is not always purely 'written' and can also make use of computer-mediated communication (CMC), so this will be covered here too.

Activity 1

Gather together various examples of writing and CMC that you or members of your family produced while at primary school (or early secondary). If you have no access to your own material, make use of what you can find in your English Language textbook and any additional material you have used in class.

Group the material into different categories and look for similarities and differences in the material under some of the following headings.

- Genre – What kinds of texts have been produced (for example, stories, fact files, answers to questions in a worksheet format, accounts of trips and holidays)?

- Age ranges – What do you notice about work produced at different ages?

- Multimodality – Are there different kinds of writing that make use of electronic communication (for example, word processing, virtual learning environments, digital **storyboards**, social media messaging) or written texts that incorporate images (for example, cartoon strips, front pages of newspapers/magazines)?

- Contexts – Are the texts produced in different settings and how might this have influenced them (for example, in school, written at home for pleasure, used in an interaction with someone else)?

- Relationship to speaking and reading – Do the texts produced have any obvious relationship to speech? Do the texts link to what children might have read?

The more data you have, the richer and more varied your revision can be.

Key terms

Literacy: Refers primarily to reading and writing, including the new types of reading and writing that occur in digital contexts.

Storyboard: A set of images to represent the action within a moving text such as a TV programme or advertisement.

Revising key concepts for written development

A major part of doing well on questions about children's **literacy** is having a good understanding of the different ways in which children develop their skills and understanding. One very important point is to appreciate that while you are given a choice of two questions on this paper, the division between children's speech and writing is not as clear-cut as that might suggest. A good starting point is to think carefully about the transition between speech and writing. How and when does this happen? Is it a case of children at a certain age just being taught to write? Is it a smooth process? Think about your own experiences (and make use of the data you gathered earlier) and write down a few notes about this.

A number of linguists and psychologists have offered different models for explaining how literacy develops.

Activity 2

On separate paper, write a short paragraph for each of the following individuals, explaining some of their key ideas relating to children's early written language development. Is there a main focus for each of them (for example, spelling) or are their ideas applicable to most areas of the topic?

- Kroll
- Martin and Rothery
- Perera
- Goodman
- Chall

- Clay
- Christie
- Kress
- Gentry

Reading and writing

While you will not be set a separate question on children's reading development, it is an important area to consider because of the link it forms between speech and writing. Reading also plays an important role in developing an understanding of how written language works. Additionally, there is plenty of evidence that children who read more, tend to become more proficient and creative writers.

Working with data

Activity 3

The questions in Paper 1, Section B give you data sets to work with and an idea to evaluate. You will move on to some suggested approaches to the exam questions soon, but look at the short piece of data here to begin with. It is taken from the writing of a girl in Year 2 (aged seven years, two months) as part of a project on the seaside. A student has started to annotate her work, but it needs more detail. Look at the prompt questions that follow and use them to help you to add in this extra detail.

Pictures have been used.

Some of the spellings are inaccurate.

The words label the pictures.

Lots of the words are connected to the seaside.

Transliteration:

- Ruby – C (girl's name)
- candy folose
- bech ball
- surf board
- bukite
- sbads
- fish and chips
- ice crime
- burgers

Prompts

1. 'Pictures have been used' and 'The words label the pictures'. How could these be developed to make more reference to ideas about the link between different modes such as writing and drawing? Does the way the child has laid this out suggest that it is influenced by something she might have read? What genre might this kind of writing be categorised into?

2. 'Some of the spellings are inaccurate.' This is true but it's much too simplistic. Which spellings are accurate and which are not? Is there a pattern to the ones which are right and the ones which are wrong? For example, are there certain vowel sounds that she gets wrong? Are there any consonants that seem to cause problems? Also, what *is* accurate here? Remember not to just focus on errors, but to consider what a child is getting right and what this might tell us about their stage of development.

3. 'Lots of the words are connected to the seaside.' Yes, this is true but again it's very basic. On a very simple level, the words are all linked because they are part of a lexical field. They are also linked because they are presumably part of a task about the topic of the seaside, so why have these been chosen rather than other ones? Could these words be categorised grammatically too? Is that linked to the nature and genre of the task?

Children's language development: getting the balance right

The questions on children's language development are assessed using AO1 and AO2 with equal weighting. This means that in your answer you need to balance a good understanding of ideas from language study – theory, research, knowledge about how children's language develops – with focused linguistic analysis of the data provided. When you are answering exam questions, you will also need to make sure you address the idea that has been set in the task.

Activity 4

Data Set 1 on page 66 is taken from the school work of a Year 2 girl (aged seven years, three months). The class had been looking at the topic of the Victorian seaside and were asked to imagine they had taken a trip to Blackpool and to write a postcard home. Using the data and the writing space provided below, identify at least five points you could make about the girl's use of language. Try to write at least one point for each of the headings provided and quote specific examples. A transliteration of the writing has been provided beside the extract.

AO1 analysis:

Lexis and semantics – Look at the range and type of vocabulary used.

_____

_____

_____

Orthography – How have letters been formed and spellings been used?

_____

_____

_____

Discourse – How has the child made use of and understood genre conventions?

_____

_____

_____

Syntax – What grammatical structures has the child used and how do these match the normal conventions of written language?

_____

_____

_____

Data Set 1

Transliteration:

Dear Mum and dad.

I wen on a steam train to get
to the seaside wen I got
there I saw a man seling
A hokey Pokey a brout one.
I went to see punch and
Judy show. After lunch i
Went to padol in the sea.
It was nice and Cold on
A hot day. I injoyd it
At the end. I brout a
nofer hokey pokey

Love Ruby-C

(Note: a Hokey Pokey is an old-fashioned style of ice cream)

Activity 5

Along with the AO1 analysis of language, you will need to respond to the wider idea put forward in the exam question. Answer the following exam-style question. The extracts of children's writing will offer you the chance to think more about the idea and guide you through a possible approach to it.

'Children's written language development is as much a question of understanding generic conventions as it is of writing clearly and accurately.'

Referring to **Data Set 1** and **Data Set 2** in detail, and to relevant ideas from language study, evaluate this view of children's language development   **[30 marks]**

Key terms

Connective: A word that joins elements together, such as 'and' and 'or'. These are also called conjunctions.

Orthography: The spelling system.

Data Set 2 is from a different Year 2 child at the age of seven years, nine months. It was created during class work on using time **connectives** in story writing. A transliteration of the writing has been provided on page 68.

Data Set 2

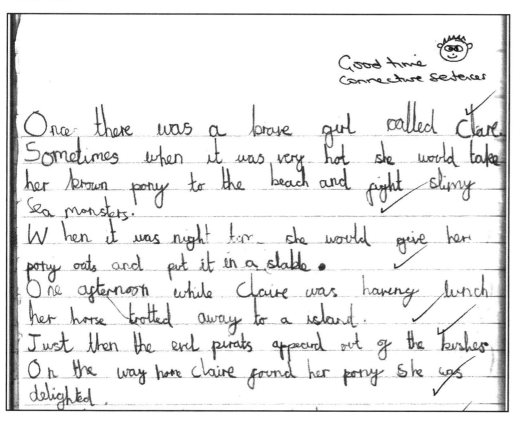

Transliteration:

Once there was a brave girl called Clare.
Sometimes when it was very hot she would take
her brown pony to the beach and fight slimy
sea monsters.
When it was night time she would give her
pony oats and put it in a stable.
One afternoon while Claire was having lunch
her horse trotted away to a island.
Just then the evil pirats appeard out of the bushes.
On the way home Claire found her pony She was
delighted.

Breaking down the question

The key to doing well on questions like the one on page 67 is to strike the right balance between the requirements of the assessment objectives and really understanding what the question is asking. First, you must identify the key terms in the idea that needs evaluating.

written language development – Think broadly about the different elements of children's writing. Use the data here to help you, but think more widely about other kinds of writing and other features you have studied.

'Children's written language development is as much a question of understanding generic conventions as it is of writing clearly and accurately.'

generic conventions – What does this term mean? Think about what is meant by genre and then think about the expectations in certain genres. Which genres do you have in these data sets? What other genres have you looked at? Have you studied any theory or case studies about genre?

writing clearly and accurately – What is meant by this? Is it about lineation, spelling and letter formation? Is it about choosing appropriate vocabulary and using accurate syntax? Is it all of these and more?

Analysing multimodal texts

When looking at the writing children produce in CMC texts, many of the same analytical tools are available to you as with traditional written texts, but it is also worth considering the ways in which the affordances of technology can add new dimensions.

Activity 6

Data Set 3 on page 70 is made up of four slides produced by a nine-year-old for a class presentation on cities around the world. (She chose Rio de Janeiro.) Read and study the data set, then answer these questions, adding as much detail as you can.

1. What genre does the text fit into and how can you tell?

_____

_____

_____

_____

2. How does the child use the affordances of technology to develop the text's meanings?

_____

_____

_____

_____

_____

_____

3. What limitations connected to the technology might have influenced some of the language in the text?

_____

_____

_____

_____

_____

_____

Data Set 3

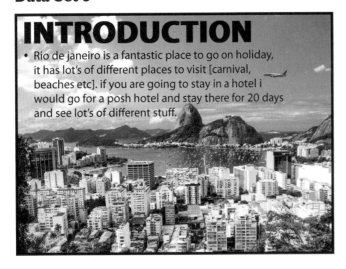

INTRODUCTION

- Rio de janeiro is a fantastic place to go on holiday, it has lot's of different places to visit [carnival, beaches etc]. if you are going to stay in a hotel i would go for a posh hotel and stay there for 20 days and see lot's of different stuff.

HOTELS TO STAY IN

Swimming pool

- Here is one some swimming pool you can go to.
- But you can to to lot's of different ones.
- This is a beautiful swimming pool to go to.

Football

- The world cup is going to be played in Brazil this year. Here are some pictures containing the Brazil squad, key player, Brazil flag.
- Neymar has two numbers 11,10
- https://www.youtube.com/watch?v=2bfp3TZHUzY

Writing by older children

The upper age limit for questions on children's language development is 11, so it is useful to look at work by pre-teens in preparation for the exam. While there will still be plenty to say about data produced by older children, it might require a slightly different approach to analysis. The writing might be more grammatically developed, contain fewer errors and inconsistencies in spelling, have a wider vocabulary and might exhibit more understanding of different genres. Again, writing by older children that has been produced using CMC might offer different angles to explore.

Activity 7

Data Set 4 is the opening of a story written by a girl in Year 7 (Aged 11 years, 11 months) using Wattpad (an online platform for young people to write and share their writing with others).

Read the data and then answer the following questions on separate paper. They will help you to focus on approaches that might be different to those you have been using on younger children's writing.

1. What evidence is there that the author is capable of using sophisticated expression and clear grammatical structure?

2. How has the writer attempted to capture an old-fashioned style and how successful is this?

3. What evidence is there of an understanding of wider cultural reference points?

4. How has the writer made use of the affordances of CMC in writing this piece?

Data Set 4

wattpad   Discover   Create   Community   Search Stories & People

The third day of November in the year of our lord, 1865, shortly before sunrise.

Hello, dear reader. My name is Grace Willow. I am sixteen years old today. And as if I'm ever going to forget it. I've been watching them, the girls in our village. They turn sixteen and become their own person. They leave home, move to the city, find someone, marry, have children, they die happy. Of course, I'm not psychic – I don't want to be burnt alive with the witches! But being a lady comes with it's drawbacks. I can't just wait for my soul-mate to appear, I have to find one. Mother says I have to marry before I turn seventeen or she'll dissenherit me!

To be perfectly honest, I wouldn't mind except I'm so terrified I'll end up in the workhouse! I drove past it in the carriage once. It fair broke my heart to see the tiny infants with their poor shaved heads, being forced to work themselves to death.

Father took me to the theatre some months ago. We stood in the stands and watched Eliza Doolittle slowly become a fine young lady. Father cheered at the end. I felt like weeping. Why on earth did dear Eliza want to become a lady? Why on earth would anyone want to be a lady? I cannot confide in anyone without Mother finding out!

That's why I am writing this diary. I so hope that nobody sneaks into my chambers and takes this. Woe betide me if they do!

Anyway, today is my sixteenth birthday and Mother and Father are hosting a masked ball to celebrate. All the important members of society are coming, so I'm told. How is that supposed to make me feel better, though? Knowing that the moment I walk through the door tonight, there will be 50 men watching me like hawks, intent on claiming the Duchess of Cambridge's daughter for their own does not inspire me at all!

Alas, I must stop writing now for Rosa is coming to dress me and as she is in charge of me, it would not do to have her show this to Mother.

Lady Grace Willow.

Language diversity and change – introduction

What does Paper 2 involve?

Paper 2 lasts 2 hours and 30 minutes and is split into two sections.

Section A: Diversity and change

Section A of the Paper 2 exam involves a choice of *two* questions. You must select *one* from either the area of language diversity *or* language change.

Question 1 deals with language diversity and Question 2 deals with language change. It is up to you to select the most useful and relevant knowledge from the topic areas you have studied.

Each question will use a wording that asks you to evaluate an idea related to change or diversity.

For example:

> Evaluate the idea that men and women use language differently.
>
> **[30 marks]**

> Evaluate the idea that the English language is deteriorating.
>
> **[30 marks]**

Section B: Language discourses

In this part of the exam paper you are given two compulsory questions, Question 3 and Question 4.

Question 3, analysing opinion pieces

Question 3 presents you with two texts on the same (or very similar) theme about language change and/or diversity in which opinions and views are put forward. An example of the question wording is given here (**X** represents what the two texts are about):

> Analyse how language is used in **Text A** and **Text B** to present views about **X**. In your answer you should:
>
> • examine any similarities and differences you find between the two texts
>
> • explore how effectively the texts present their views.
>
> **[40 marks]**

What will the Question 3 texts be like?

The texts will be drawn from a range of contemporary writing for non-specialist audiences, but they will always be about language change or diversity (possibly with some overlap). You might be given online or newspaper articles, extracts from books, letters or online comments, or other kinds of writing in which opinions are put forward. You can revise this by making sure you have read a range of these texts on different topics.

Question 4: writing opinion pieces

Question 4 of Paper 2 is another compulsory question and it asks you to produce a piece of your own opinion-based writing that assesses the 'ideas and issues' raised in the two texts you have just analysed for Question 3. You must bring in ideas from language study here, so this is where the knowledge that you have learned in preparation for Section A of Paper 2 also comes in.

An example of the question wording is given here:

> Write an opinion article about **X** in which you assess the ideas and issues raised in **Text A** and **Text B** and argue your own views.
>
> **[30 marks]**

What are the topics for Paper 2?

The diversity topics you will have studied are: **gender**, **accent** and **dialect**, social class, occupation, **ethnicity** and **International Englishes**. You will have also studied the topic of language change. It is important to remember, however, that there is lots of overlap between all of these topics and it is likely that you will be drawing knowledge from a variety of different areas.

How many marks are awarded for each section?

There are 30 marks for Question 1 and Question 2 (you choose which one to answer), 40 marks for Question 3 and 30 marks for Question 4.

How long should you spend on each section?

You should spend 45 minutes on the Section A question (including at least 5 minutes for planning). For Section B, ensure you spend at least 15 minutes reading and annotating the two texts, then 45 minutes to write up your answer for Question 3. Spend 45 minutes writing your Question 4 response.

Key terms

Accent: The way that people pronounce sounds.

Dialect: A style of language used within a particular geographical region.

Ethnic identity / ethnicity: Feeling connected with people who have similar cultural backgrounds, heritage, or family ties.

Gender: The social expectations that arise as a result of being one sex or another.

International English: The idea of English as a language that is used in international contexts of all kinds.

How is Section A assessed?

Question 1 or 2

The AOs used for assessing your Question 1 or 2 response are AO1 and AO2.

- AO1: 10 marks – For this part of the exam (and unlike in Paper 1, Section A) AO1 is primarily concerned with how you shape a line of argument, how accurately you write and how you structure an academic and focused response to the task, using a suitable linguistic register.

- AO2: 20 marks – This assesses your understanding of ideas from language study, so you should be showing your detailed understanding of key concepts, studies and processes while demonstrating a clear grasp of how language works.

How is Section B assessed?

Question 3

This task is assessed using three Assessment Objectives.

- AO1: 10 marks – This assesses your ability to analyse the language used in the texts and to describe their features accurately.

- AO3: 15 marks – This is concerned with your analysis and evaluation of the meanings and representations created in the texts.

- AO4: 15 marks – Here you are assessed on how well you explore connections across the texts using a linguistic **register**.

Question 4

This task is assessed using two Assessment Objectives.

- AO2: 20 marks – As you can see, the balance here is heavily weighted towards knowledge of language concepts, so one of your main tasks is to inform the reader of some of the relevant ideas about language that you have learned on your course.

- AO5: 10 marks – Your target audience will be non-specialists, therefore you will need to explain any theory, concepts or ideas in a way that a new audience can understand. At the same time, you will need to address some of the ideas and issues raised in Texts A and B, making sure that you have a clear position to take in response to them.

> **Key term**
>
> **Register:** A form of specialist language. For example, the language of sport or science.

Issues in language and gender

There are two main aspects of language and gender.

1. Gender and representation – how men, women and their language use are talked *about* or written *about*.

2. Gender and language use – how men and women *use* language in *real* conversation.

For Section A of the Paper 2 exam you will write an essay on a theoretical area of language. When tackling a question on gender, it is important that you ensure you understand which *part* of gender the question is asking you to focus on.

For example, the following questions are rather different from one another in focus:

> Evaluate the idea that the English language remains biased towards men.
>
> **[30 marks]**

> Evaluate the idea that men use more competitive language features than women in conversation.
>
> **[30 marks]**

The first deals with bias and inequality in the language used to represent men and women, and the second deals with the idea that men supposedly use different language features to women in conversation. We will return to some exam-style questions later.

Language and gender research

In order to fulfil the AO2 requirement for the Paper 2, Section A essay, it is important that you refer to relevant theories, studies and concepts. There is a great deal of academic research that has been carried out on the area of language and gender. You will have studied some of the research discussed in this section and you may also have other research you can refer to.

Throughout this chapter you will be introduced to some new research and ideas. Language research never stands still; academics are carrying out new projects all the time, so this is an opportunity for you to evaluate research you may not be familiar with and to work out how it could fit with your existing knowledge. It is important to remember that there is not a finite list of theories and concepts you should learn or refer to; what's important is studying a range of different ideas and then selecting useful and relevant information to enable you to carefully address the question in the exam.

Tip

AO2 covers concepts, issues and theoretical understanding, but it's important that you show a clear and detailed understanding of a concept or theory rather than simply 'name-dropping' without showing any knowledge about what that theorist proposed. Try to avoid simply listing the gender theories you have learned.

Activity 1

Match the area of gender and representation on the left with the relevant examples and research on the right. There may be more than one example/research detail for each. There are also questions for you to consider, so continue this table and make additional notes on separate sheet, including any other research or your own mini-investigation work.

Gender and representation	Examples and research
Sexist language Who shrieks, nags, swaggers, strides, argues…? What are the **connotations** of such terms? What do they suggest about our attitudes to gender?	The English-speaking world has traditionally used **patronyms** – names that relate to the male line of inheritance. For example, 'son', 'Mac' and 'O' can be added to create names such as *Hodgson, MacDonald* and *O'Brien*.
Job titles How do we refer to male and female jobs? Why can these labels be seen as problematic?	Diminutive **suffixes** are used, for example, in waitress, actress.
	Hoey (2005) used the term '**lexical priming**' to describe the way in which well-used words and phrases can carry an innate gender prejudice, for example, 'a grumpy old man'.
Terms of address Consider the use of Ms, Mrs, Miss. What about address terms such as 'sweetpea', 'honey pie', 'chief', 'boss'? Who do these refer to and what do they mean? Are these problematic?	Muriel Schulz (1975) suggested that pairs of words that would normally be seen as equivalents often exhibit asymmetry when they are about gender. Examples include madam/sir, bachelor/spinster, wizard/witch. What other examples are there and what are the connotations of the male and female terms in each pair?
	We often hear terms such as 'mankind', 'manning a stall' and 'two-man tent'.
	The terms Ms, Mrs and Miss reveal society's social attitudes towards gender and marital status, including the notion that gender is binary.
Gendered pronouns and false generics Using 'man' and 'he' to refer to both genders. What terms can you think of and how could this use of language be viewed as problematic?	Hines (1994) states that women are often referred to as desserts (cupcake, sweet, tart). What other semantic fields can you think of that can be applied to the way in which men and women are referred to?
	Other societies, such as Iceland, use **matronyms** (the mother's first name) plus the term for daughter or son.
	In Spain children can inherit names from both of their parents to create surnames with multiple meanings. In Sweden no titles are used at all, just people's first names and surnames.
Marked terms We tend to use terms such as 'lady doctor', 'male nurse', 'male prostitute', 'woman pilot'. What does this tell us about these job roles?	Does language reflect or determine the way we think? The **Sapir-Whorf hypothesis** is concerned with the idea that the language we use determines the way we view the world. How have some people attempted to address this?
Lexical asymmetry Some pairs of words that relate to males and females may seem to be equal but they are often not. How could this be problematic?	Examples include 'wolf', 'vixen', 'minx', 'kitten', 'dog', 'moose'.
	Many terms in English are marked for gender. For example, the term 'family man' marks out a man who spends time with his family (suggesting that the norm might be those who do not).

Gendered discourses

Discourses play a part in representing gender. These are ways of talking about and describing gender and can range from 'common sense' representations of gender roles or more overtly sexist representations of particular women (usually) or men (occasionally). An example might be this gendered discourse surrounding female politicians in *The Daily Mail* recently, or these references to female celebrities in the *Mail Online*'s sidebar.

Key terms

Connotation: The associations that we have for a word or phrase.

Lexical priming: The way in which some words appear to be ready-made for certain meanings, as a result of their habitual use in the same contexts.

Matronyms: Names that reflect female lines of inheritance.

Patronyms: Names that reflect male lines of inheritance.

Sapir-Whorf hypothesis: The idea, derived from the work of Edward Sapir and Benjamin Lee Whorf, that our language constructs our view of the world and that it is difficult or even impossible to think beyond it.

Suffix: A particle added to the end of a word.

Text A

Text B

DON'T MISS

▶ Chloe Green displays post-baby body…

▶ Gemma Collins showcases her killer curves…

▶ Rita Ora puts on an eye-popping display in two neon swimsuits as she frolics on a yacht in sunny Barcelona

---

Activity 2

Carry out a short language analysis on Text A and Text B by annotating the texts using the language levels (see page 9). Make notes on how the texts present particular discourses around women.

Activity 3

In 2017 the campaign group Let Toys Be Toys carried out a survey of toy catalogues aimed at children (http://lettoysbetoys.org.uk/toy-catalogues-2017). They found the following.

• Boys were four times as likely to be shown playing with cars.
• 97% of children shown with guns and war toys were boys.
• Girls were nearly twice as likely to be shown with kitchens or other domestic play items.
• Girls were nearly seven times as likely to be shown in caring or nurturing play.
• Girls were 12 times as likely to be shown playing with baby dolls (rising to 50 times excluding the Early Learning Centre catalogue).
• Boys were almost twice as likely to be shown with construction toys.
• Girls were twice as likely to be shown with art and craft toys.

1. Why might these visual representations of gendered behaviour be significant to a wider discussion of how language represents gender? Write your answer on separate paper.

2. Look at the four short explanations of ideas about language presented below. How might these ideas, used with some of the examples and concepts on page 77, help you explain why language is important in representing gender? On a separate piece of paper, write some notes.

   • Sapir and Whorf: the Sapir-Whorf hypothesis suggests that language controls or influences thought. If language can do this (and there are significant counter-arguments) then it follows that language might shape attitudes towards (among other things) gender. Language matters.

   • Loftus: Elizabeth Loftus's work on eyewitness testimony (1975) suggests that language can affect people's recall of events. Again, language is seen to influence how we think and respond.

   • Miller and Swift (1977): these two influential writers argued that sexist language obscures clear communication and should be reformed. Many of their suggestions – for example, to use gender-neutral terms such as 'chairperson' and 'humanity' (for 'chairman' and 'mankind') – have since become the norm in formal written publications and style guides. But is this kind of **language reform** enough?

   • Blatt (2017) and Hunt (2017): both looked at how authors of popular fiction (Blatt) and children's fiction (Hunt) used verbs to describe characters' speech, discovering that male characters often 'ordered', 'shouted' and 'chuckled' while female characters 'begged', 'murmured' and 'wept'.

3. On separate paper, write a plan for an essay using the following question:

> 'Evaluate the idea that women and men are represented differently through language.'
>
> **[30 marks]**

Key term

Language reform: A term used, usually by liberal commentators, to support the idea of consciously changing language because it is considered unfair to different groups.

Activity 4

Look at the boxes opposite. Match the area of gender and spoken language on the left with the relevant examples and research on the right. There may be more than one example/research detail for each. You could continue this table on paper to add any of your own ideas or your own mini-investigation work.

Gender and language use	Examples and research
Early work on language and gender tended to represent women's language as inferior to men's.	In the 1990s Deborah Tannen published her book *You Just Don't Understand*. She represents male and female language using a series of six contrasts such as status versus support, where men are thought to use language to gain and keep status and to be more competitive, whereas women are thought to use language to gain confirmation and support for their ideas.
The idea that language variation is more about our role and position in society than our gender. Traditionally men have held more dominant roles so their language was considered to be more dominant.	Robin Lakoff (1975) wrote the book *Language and Woman's Place* where she noted some key female language traits such as hedges, empty adjectives, super-polite forms, hyper-correct grammar and indirect requests.
	Eckert (1989) carried out the famous 'Jocks and Burnouts' study. She defined groups in terms of the social practices the speakers engaged in and her results showed that those who share social practices tend to use similar forms of language.
The idea that men and women are socialised differently from childhood so they use language differently.	Dale Spender (1980) identifies power with a male patriarchal order.
The idea that there are not innate differences in language use but rather we 'perform', play a role and construct our gendered identities through the language we use. Gender is not something you are; it's something you do.	O'Barr and Atkins (1980) studied courtroom cases and witnesses' speech. They reported that language differences were based on context, situation and roles rather than gender. Their findings showed that both males and females used powerless language in some contexts, therefore females didn't use powerless language simply because they were women; they used it because of their position in a given context.
	Tannen's ideas about males and females were that they are socialised into seeing themselves as having very different roles and positions in life and therefore the language they use reflects this.
The idea that gender is just one aspect of our identities. The idea of social practice is concerned with a group of people using language for shared activities and mutual goals.	Otto Jesperson (1922) argued that male language forms were 'the norm' and the language of others was 'deficient'. Early research into language and gender tended to present findings in this way.
	Janet Hyde (2005) proposed a 'gender similarities hypothesis' claiming that there are many more similarities than differences in the language that men and women use and many differences are more to do with other variables such as class, age, occupation and sexuality.
	Deborah Cameron challenges the notion of there being innate differences in the language used by men and women. She believes that we cannot base ideas about gender on sociological assumptions, such as 'men have a natural desire to be competitive'. Instead, she focuses on how speakers construct and perform their gendered identities for themselves.
	In her 1990 book *Gender Trouble* Judith Butler suggests that gender is 'performative'.

Key terms

Case study: An in-depth study of a single context that can be used to offer insights for further studies or other cases.

Community of practice: A group of people who share understandings, perspectives and forms of language use as a result of meeting regularly over time.

Using theoretical ideas in your Paper 2, Section A essay

In order to reach Level 3 in the mark scheme for AO2, you need to show your examiner you have a 'detailed knowledge of linguistic ideas, concepts and research'. The theories and concepts you discuss must, of course, be relevant to the statement in the question and it is up to you to consider the body of research that is most useful to help answer the question.

If you are able to begin linking research to other studies and use an integrated approach, then you are beginning to move up to Level 4: 'identifying and commenting on different views, approaches and interpretations of linguistic issues'. Here you need to try and show the examiner that you can bring ideas together and that you can explore the research, identifying contextual factors and wider variables such as age, social group, ethnicity and so on. Level 5 in the mark scheme involves a succinct analysis and evaluation throughout, showing a 'conceptualised overview'. You must 'evaluate and challenge' ideas, so you need to be critical of approaches and findings. You need to be able to critically evaluate theories, showing you understand the more recent ways of thinking, for example, concerning performativity, **communities of practice** and identity.

Communities of practice

Research has moved on since the early studies of language and gender, and most researchers agree it is useful to examine inter-speaker differences and who is connected to who in a community. When considering communities of practice, we can examine who shares social practice with who; it's not just about connectivity, it's about the quality of that connectivity. Examples of communities of practice could be a workplace, a sports club, a book club, online gamers, social media friends, student societies, parenting groups or church groups.

 Stretch

Record a conversation from one of your social groups and transcribe it. Analyse how language is used by the speakers. Write a **case study** of a community of practice that you are part of. Where relevant, it can be useful to refer to your own research in your Paper 2, Section A exam answer.

Activity 5

Penny Eckert carried out a classic study where she examined two groups of high school students – the 'Jocks' and the 'Burnouts'.

What did Eckert's research reveal about social practices and language use? One point has been made for you. Try and list three more.

- In order to explain variation, it is useful to analyse communities more closely. This prevents over-generalisation and allows us to explore inter-speaker differences more closely.

- _____

- _____

- _____

Activity 6

Think about the activities and groups that you are part of. To what extent is there a shared linguistic practice? Use the levels of analysis table on page 9 and list some typical language features that you may use with your different social groups. Copy and complete a table like the one below.

Social group	Typical language features

Stretch

Read and summarise Lucy Jones' work on a specific community of practice: a lesbian hiking group. You can find a journal article which summarises her work at: https://www.academia.edu/536616/_The_only_dykey_one_Constructions_of_in_authenticity_in_a_lesbian_community_of_practice.

This community of practice consisted of older middle-class white women and she examined how they presented and constructed their identity by looking at what it means to be a lesbian in this **social group**. She found that they co-constructed their identity using labelling strategies such as 'butch' to reject the stereotypical femme identity (which was thought to reinforce the patriarchy). They also used words such as 'dykey' in a positive way and 'girly' in a negative way to refer to what they thought was an inauthentic style of lesbian. What's important about this study is that it shows us that there is more than one 'version' of lesbian identity, just as there's more than one 'version' of being a woman.

Key term

Social group: Individuals who share interests and connections with others, or who are classified as having something in common.

Key terms

Pejoration: A process whereby a word or phrase develops more negative connotations. For example, 'cunning' used to mean knowledgeable.

Stereotype: The idea that whole groups of people conform to the same, limited, range of characteristics.

Stretch

Read Emma Moore's work on communities of practice at: http://linguistics-research-digest. blogspot.co.uk/search?q=eden.

Moore focused her analysis on the language of schoolgirls in a local high school in Bolton and was interested in the use of non-standard 'were', for example, 'I were happy' and 'She were excited'. Read about Moore's work and produce your own summary of her findings. Can you link Moore's findings to any other research you have studied?

Heteronormativity and feminism

Heteronormativity refers to the belief that it is 'natural' or 'normal' to be heterosexual. This is clearly problematic and this bias causes people to believe that non-heterosexual people are somehow different, leading to negative **stereotypes**. This can then enable homophobic discourse.

Activity 7

We face a number of problematic issues living in a heteronormative society. Some of these issues are listed below. Expand on each point by identifying some of your own examples that might relate to your own experiences.

- Many people are marginalised as they don't fit society's expectations. This had led to the process of *semantic derogation* of certain groups (using language negatively to put groups down) and in turn the **pejoration** of words (where words take on more negative meanings) such as 'gay' and 'queer' (incidentally, 'queer' has now been reclaimed and is a scholarly concept of linguistic study).

_____

_____

_____

_____

_____

_____

- People assume the language used by gay men or lesbians is used *only* by them and that *all* gay men and lesbians speak in the same way. There is an assumption that there is a gay language and certain linguistic features can be labelled as 'gay' just because gay and lesbian people happen to use them.

_____

_____

_____

_____

_____

- Explicit homophobia still exists, for example, the use of 'fag' in American high schools to insult homosexual males.

_____

_____

_____

_____

_____

- Implicit homophobia is used in the media, for example, we see headlines such as 'X admits he's gay' and 'X in hiding after telling the world he's gay'. In the first example, the verb 'admits' has connotations of 'coming clean' or confessing to wrong-doing and it tends to be associated with deviant behaviour. In the second example, 'in hiding' suggests he has something to be ashamed of.

_____

_____

_____

_____

_____

- People often only talk as if there are two sexualities – gay or straight. This means that bisexuality and other sexual orientations are often erased from our discourse.

_____

_____

_____

_____

_____

Stretch

There has been recent research into language and transgender identity. There is an ideological expectation of 'authentic' trans identity. For example, we expect transgender males to fit into the 'normal' gendered pattern of male identity by having relationships with women and being very masculine in their appearance and behaviour. Lucy Jones at the University of Nottingham has recently carried out an analysis of the two most popular trans vloggers. She introduces the concept of 'transnormativity' – the idea that it is thought there should be a normative behaviour concerning trans identity. You can read Jones' work at: https://www.academia.edu/19573951/Discourses_of_transnormativity_in_vloggers_ identity_construction.

Stretch

Research Barrett's 1995 study on gay men and drag (see *Language and Gender: A Reader*, edited by Coates and Pichler, Wiley-Blackwell, 2011). Barrett examined how African American drag queens used language to 'play act' at being women. He found that the gay men, in the context of their performance, stereotyped white women's language and many of the language features used could be linked to Lakoff's supposed 'women's language features'.

Read the article at: http://citeseerx.ist.psu.edu/viewdoc/download?doi=10.1.1.483.3659& rep=rep1&type=pdf.

Think about how gender and ethnicity is marked in drag performance. Barrett found that when performing their drag identities, the men used a mixture of African American English (AAVE) features, features that were thought to be stereotypically gay speech features, and features of upper-middle-class white women's language.

Podesva: the use of falsetto in constructing a persona

Researchers are becoming more interested in the area of language and sexuality. An example of this is Podesva's 2007 study into the use of falsetto by a gay male in constructing his persona. Falsetto is a specific voice quality, involving a rapid vocal fold vibration with a very high pitch. The use of falsetto among men is thought to be a socially marked behaviour and may be involved in the performance of a stereotypically 'camp' gay identity.

Podesva recorded one (out) gay male named Heath in three different contexts, as Podesva was interested in cross-situational variation. The contexts were:

- a barbecue with gay friends

- a conversation with his father

- a meeting at work.

	At a BBQ with gay friends	During a conversation with his father	At a meeting at work
Falsetto utterances (N)	35	10	15
Total utterances (N)	386	260	403
Percentage falsetto utterances (%)	9.07	3.85	3.72

Podesva found that Heath used falsetto most in the barbecue setting. Not only was his falsetto more frequent, it was also longer in duration, higher in pitch and involved a wider pitch range. Podesva found that falsetto was used to construct social meaning and the feature allowed Heath to be more expressive with friends. Podesva believed that Heath used it to construct one of his personae, namely a flamboyant 'diva' persona and that falsetto may also have helped to build his gay identity.

Therefore, Podesva argues that falsetto is used for expressive purposes: to signal emotion. Expressiveness tends to be linked to femininity in society, so if gay males are using features (such as falsetto) to be more expressive, in turn, gay male identity tends to be associated with femininity. Podesva's work suggests that there is no such thing as a gay feature; rather features can take on gay meaning via associations. Moreover, it is impossible to say that certain language features have an associated meaning, but rather when language features are used often enough, they tend to take on certain associations and therefore meanings.

Activity 8

How does Podesva's work fit with other studies you have previously looked at? How can Podesva's work add weight to your knowledge about language and identity? Write a short summary explaining the connections.

_____

_____

_____

_____

_____

_____

_____

_____

_____

_____

_____

_____

_____

_____

_____

_____

Stretch

Podesva also examined the use of creaky voice (more informally known as 'vocal fry'). There have been various studies into vocal fry (which is characteristically the opposite of falsetto as it involves slow rather than rapid vibration of the vocal cords). Read the blog post about vocal fry by Mark Liberman at: http://languagelog.ldc.upenn.edu/nll/?p=3626.

Key term

Vocal fry: A vocal effect where the speaker produces a rasping, creaky sound by blowing air through the vocal cords.

Language, gender and sexuality: performativity

In recent years, there has been a shift from viewing language as *reflecting* gender to viewing language as *constructing* gender. It is now widely accepted that gender is performative rather than innate; we construct and perform our gender and we do this, in part, through the language we use.

In her book *Gender Trouble*, which details the way in which we *trouble* gender when we do anything out of the ordinary in terms of our language, Judith Butler shows us how our identity emerges through interaction. She puts forward the idea that gender is a fluid concept and it changes according to the context we are in. We often engage in certain gendered traits (women wearing make-up, for example). When these gendered traits are repeated over and over, they become naturalised and they are then seen as part of 'normal' reality.

Clearly, we are not the same person in every context. For example, if you work in a restaurant, you present yourself as a professional server, but with friends, you most likely present yourself very differently. For instance, you may perform a masculine identity when watching football with friends by, for example, using expletives to show anger after an own goal, but in another context, you may use expletives to create humour, thus performing a very different identity. Not all language features point to the same identity and we continue to vary our language to construct the identity we wish to project.

Activity 9

1. Drawing on your own identity, list some traits that you consider to be typical of your gender and some traits that may be considered less typical. What kind of language might you use to perform your gender and how might this change in different contexts? Add some thoughts below.

_____

_____

_____

_____

_____

_____

_____

2. On separate paper, write a plan for an essay in response to the following exam-style question:

> Evaluate the idea that our identity is created through the language we use.
>
> **[30 marks]**

Regional variation

Activity 1

The terms 'accent' and 'dialect' are clearly different. Start this unit by revising what these terms refer to. Write your definitions below:

Accent: _____

Dialect: _____

Received Pronunciation (RP) has historically been considered the accent with the highest prestige because it was socially approved. RP is sometimes referred to as **non-regional** because it is spoken all over the UK; it is not linked to a specific region. It tends to be associated with a more privileged social class. The term **Standard English** is associated with written language and is the agreed standard for writing. In lots of spoken contexts, non-standard forms are used. It is generally accepted that Standard English is the appropriate dialect in which to write in formal contexts. However, in spoken language and in some written texts (such as CMC texts) regional forms are entirely appropriate.

It is important to remember that regional speech features are different from the natural features of spoken language that everyone uses (refer to the mind map you completed on page 26).

Tip

Mind maps are a useful way to organise your ideas. You may wish to produce a mind map for each theoretical area you study and then put them all together to identify areas of theory that might overlap or link together.

Key terms

Non-regional: An alternative name for the **RP** accent.

Received Pronunciation (RP): An accent traditionally associated with high social status. 'Received' refers to the idea of social acceptance in official circles.

Slang: Language that is used in informal contexts and widely recognised (unlike dialect usage, which occurs only in particular regions).

Standard English: A language system that acts as an agreed common language, especially for formal uses. This primarily refers to the writing system of English.

Activity 2

Examine the examples on page 88 and tick the correct box to identify whether the feature is:

- a general aspect of connected speech or an informal usage that is widely recognised (a **slang** term)

- a feature that shows regional variation.

Some of the examples may contain aspects of both, so use the boxes to make some careful notes about the examples. The first one has been done for you.

Example	A general aspect of connected speech or a widely used slang term	A feature that shows regional variation
'I was gonna go out but I was too tired'	✓ The speaker is using elision here by merging together the verb phrase 'going to'. This is a completely normal feature of natural discourse and is widely used.	
'You out tonight?'		
'We was really angry about it'		
'erm (.) I dunno'		
'What do you fink about it?'		
'I goes, "no way, man!"'		
'Are we meetin' up tomorrow (.) I mean on Friday?'		
'I was like (.) so excited!'		
'Give us a kiss!'		
'Are yous comin'?'		
'That's amazeballs!'		

Right or wrong? Correct or incorrect?

Because we make judgements about language, we tend to use the words 'right', 'wrong', 'correct' and 'incorrect' to describe regional varieties of English. As linguistic descriptivists, you should avoid these kinds of prescriptive, judgemental comments.

Activity 3

Revise the terms 'prescriptivism' and 'descriptivism' and write definitions below.

Prescriptivism: _____

Descriptivism: _____

Lexical and semantic variation

Most regional varieties contain dialect vocabulary (variation in words and their meanings). While we can use lots of different words to express the same thing, the same word can also be used to mean different things and this variation can be down to the region you live in. For example, 'right' can be employed not only to indicate direction or agreement, but in some dialects it can also be used as an intensifier in the sense of 'very'. In Yorkshire, it is common to hear the phrase 'it were right good'.

> **Tip**
>
> It is useful to add examples to your Paper 2, Section A essay to show the examiner you understand some of the different kinds of language variation.

Activity 4

Copy and complete the mind map by listing as many additional senses of the word 'solid' as you can think of. Produce further mini mindmaps to note down the senses of 'heavy', 'cool', 'dark' and 'deep'.

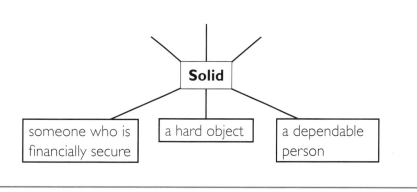

This variation is often regional, although other factors may also come into effect, such as the person's age and the social group they belong to.

Activity 5

Complete the following tasks on separate paper.

1. In what way could this kind of lexical and semantic variation be seen as problematic? For example, is it a problem that speakers use different words for the same concept or the same words to refer to different concepts? Write a paragraph to explain your ideas.

2. What value does regional vocabulary have for its speakers? Write a paragraph to explain your ideas.

Grammatical variation

Another way linguists describe regional variation is according to differences in grammar and syntax. Again, there are very different attitudes to dialect grammar and comments such as 'standards are slipping' are often used when referring to dialect grammar. When we examine the history of dialect grammar, we can see that Standard English itself is a dialect that happens to be the 'approved' and prestigious form. It becomes clear that it's impossible to use terms such as right and wrong when referring to regional variation.

Key terms

Accent variation: The way that pronunciations vary between different speakers, or the variations a single speaker might produce in different contexts.

Determiner: Determiners, as the name suggests, help to determine what a noun refers to. Determiners can be wide ranging in their reference, including quantity ('some', 'many'), definiteness ('the' or 'a'), possession ('my', 'our') and demonstrativeness ('these', 'those'). Demonstratives are also called deictics, or pointing words.

Preposition: A word that typically indicates direction, position, or relationship, such as 'into', 'on', or 'of '.

Relativiser: Another word for a relative pronoun, for example, 'which', 'who', 'that', often used at the front of a subordinate clause.

Activity 6

Revise some of the major word classes where dialect variation commonly exists. Use your class notes, a textbook and knowledge of your own or other dialects to help you identify some grammatical variation that still exists today. On separate paper, copy out the headings listed below and add notes under each, including examples. You may also be able to identify which dialects use these particular forms. One example has been started for you.

- **Prepositions**: Prepositions are often used differently. For example, in some northern regions of England, the preposition 'while' is often used to replace the Standard English 'until' and phrases such as 'I'm working two while six' are commonly heard.

- Pronouns

- The verb 'to be', for example, the use of 'was' and 'were' with different pronouns

- Other verb forms

- The use of **determiners**, for example, 'those' and 'them'

- Double negatives

- **Relativisers**, for example, the use of 'what' instead of 'that' or 'which' to join clauses

Activity 7

1. Complete the table below to match up the regional non-standard English feature with the example in the second column.

2. Next, analyse the examples in more detail. In the third column explain why the regional form is linguistically different from Standard English. One example has been done for you.

Non-standard English feature	Example	Analysis
Plural pronoun being used as singular	the book what I read	
Irregular verbs being regularised	down the shops	
Different use of adverbials	I never saw nothing	
Different use of determiners	them people	
Multiple negation	I seed you	
'What' used as a relativiser	Give us a biscuit	In this imperative, the first person plural pronoun 'us' is being used to refer to one person.

Accent variation

Phonological variation deals with the use of accent features. There is a vast amount of variation in the types of vowels and consonants used in British accents and you will be familiar with the phonemic alphabet which is commonly used to transcribe the phonemes or sounds that a speaker makes.

Activity 8

The phonemic alphabet is based on the RP accent; other accents are described as being different from RP. What problems might this cause for some regional speakers? Why is it important that we treat regional varieties fairly? On separate paper, write a paragraph or two with your ideas.

Stretch

Interview some older members of your community about their language use. Are there any specific features of language that they can recognise as being different from the way other people (perhaps younger people) use language? Are there any forms of language that they consider specific to their age group?

Tip

Use websites of local and national newspapers to find articles reporting on regional accents and dialects. Carefully read the articles and identify the views that are being put forward. This is also very good practice for Paper 2, Section B in which you could be given two articles on accent and dialect to analyse and compare.

Activity 9

Revise the broad differences between northern and southern varieties of English. For example, how would each set of speakers say the words 'bus' and 'castle'? Use the phonemic alphabet to transcribe these words and any other distinctions you are familiar with in a table like the one below.

Northern pronunciations	Southern pronunciations

Activity 10

What other accent variations are you familiar with? Make notes on the following usages by giving definitions and examples of each of the following.

Glottal stops _____

Post-vocalic /r/ _____

Substitution of /ŋ/ _____

Stretch

Listen to some examples of different accents and dialects from The British Library: Survey of English Dialects: https://sounds.bl.uk/Accents-and-dialects/Survey-of-English-dialects/.

Have a go at transcribing a section and analyse the features that are specific to that particular variety.

People often have very strong and negative attitudes towards accents. For example, the substitution of the final /ŋ/ for a /n/ in words such as 'giving' is often described as sloppy or lazy speech. While it is often referred to as 'g' dropping, this is inaccurate, as for many speakers, there was no /g/ there in the first place. It is problematic that people often think about written language rather than spoken language when discussing differences and this only adds to the negative attitudes about regional varieties.

Key terms

Covert prestige: Status gained from peer group recognition, rather than public acknowledgement.

Overt prestige: Status that is publicly acknowledged.

Activity 11

Remind yourself about why it is inaccurate to call the above variations lazy or sloppy. It may be helpful to revise the terms '**covert prestige**' and '**overt prestige**' to help you explain differences.

Activity 12

Why do regional forms continue to be used if they are socially stigmatised? Why doesn't everyone try to use the prestige variety? Has society changed in terms of class distinctions? Are there changing attitudes towards RP and regional varieties? Write some notes on separate paper exploring these ideas.

Activity 13

Examine the examples in the table below and tick whether the accent is RP or a regional pronunciation. If it is a regional pronunciation, use some terms to identify how it's different from the RP pronunciation. One row has been completed for you.

Example written in Standard English	Phonemic transcription	RP pronunciation	Regional pronunciation and analysis
take	/tek/		✓ A common pronunciation used in northern English accents, such as Sheffield English. The diphthong [eɪ] is changed to a single vowel [e].
thief	/tiːf/		
path	/pɑːθ/		
pub	/pʊb/		
horse	/ɔːs/		
got to	/gɒrə/		
thinking	/fɪnkɪn/		
hair	/heə/		

Activity 14

Choose a regional accent – it could be your own or one used in a TV programme or film. On separate paper, note down some words that contain features of that accent then transcribe them using the phonemic alphabet.

Language and social class

There has been lots of research into the effect that social class has on language use. For example, Labov's New York Department Store Study (1966) concluded that differences in the production of the post-vocalic 'r' could be linked to social class, and in his Norwich Study (1974), Trudgill found a link between a speaker's social class and the pronunciation of nasal and velar nasal sounds.

Activity 15

Early studies such as those by Labov and Trudgill relied on a categorising system for social class that would now be considered rather outdated.

On separate paper, outline in more detail the research methods and results of these two studies. What was the traditional system for categorising a person's social class and how could this be seen as problematic?

Linguistic research has moved on since the 1970s and there are now more modern methods of establishing social class. There are online tests such as The Great British Class Calculator and researchers take into account a number of key factors such as household income, the kinds of people you mix with and the cultural activities you engage in.

It is clear that while class may be a factor that has some influence on the language we use, it is impossible to say that one factor alone, such as class or accent, determines the way we speak. Milroy's Belfast study (1987) adopted a different approach. She based her work on the theory of **social networks**.

Activity 16

Use separate paper to recap Milroy's research methods and findings. You could use class notes to help you. Revise the terms '**density**' and '**multiplexity**' and use them in your description of Milroy's work.

As you have seen in the communities of practice section in *Paper 2, Section A: Language, gender and sexuality* (pages 75–86), the most recent way of thinking takes the approach that the social practices we engage in have the most significant influence on our language use. For example, Eckert's work with American high school students has been particularly influential and other studies, such as Moore's Bolton study, follow the community of practice approach.

Key terms

Density: In studies of social networks, density refers to the number of connections that people have.

Multiplexity: In studies of social networks, multiplexity refers to the number of ways in which two individuals might relate to each other, for example, as friends, workmates and family members.

Social network: A network of relations between people in their membership of different groups.

Stretch

Explore the spoken language data in the following websites. Listen to examples from both male and female speakers of different ages and write down any observations you make.

- Talk of The Toon at http://research.ncl. ac.uk/decte/toon/

- British Library 'Sounds Familiar' website at http://www.bl.uk/ learning/langlit/sounds/

- The International Corpus of English at http://ice-corpora.net/ ice/sounds.htm

Activity 17

Think about your own language and the language of those around you. Do you believe your language reflects your social class or does your community of practice have more influence on the way you use language? On separate paper, write a paragraph explaining your ideas.

Activity 18

A number of key studies have been carried out into accent, dialect and social class. On separate paper, create a summary table for those listed below to remind yourself of some of these key studies, their methodologies and their results. Evaluate each study and identify other areas the study could link to.

You may have also carried out some research of your own. Your own mini-investigations are equally valid, so you could draw on these when addressing the Paper 2, Section A question in the exam.

Include more rows in your table to add other studies you may have read about or conducted yourself. You could use headings such as: 'What was of interest?', 'What was the **methodology**?', 'What were the results?', 'What does this tell us about language?' and 'What other studies could I link this to?'

- Labov's New York Department Store Study (1966)
- Labov's Martha's Vineyard Study (1963)
- Cheshire's Reading Study (1982)
- Trudgill's Norwich Study (1974)
- Work on **Multicultural London English**
- Work on **Estuary English**
- Work on **dialect levelling**
- Giles' work on attitudes to accents (1970s) and his **matched guise technique** tests
- Giles' Communication Accommodation Theory (CAT) and his ideas about **convergence** and **divergence**
- Bernstein's **Restricted** and **Elaborated Code**
- Milroy and Milroy's Belfast Studies (1978–)
- Lave and Wenger's concept of a Community of Practice (1991)

Key terms

Convergence: In language study, changing one's language in order to move towards that of another individual.

Dialect levelling: The way in which dialect terms have been dropping out of use.

Divergence: In language study, changing one's language in order to move away from that of another individual.

Elaborated code: An idea advanced by Bernstein (and much disputed) that middle-class speakers use context-free, complex forms of language.

Estuary English: A recent accent variety used in south-east England which combines RP with some aspects of regional southern accents. 'Estuary' refers to the Thames Estuary area.

Matched guise technique: An experimental technique where a single actor puts on a different accent for different audiences, but keeps the content of the speech the same.

Methodology: The study of different ways to research ideas.

Multicultural London English: A recent variety combining elements of the language of different ethnic groups, particularly Afro-Caribbean English. The variety arose in London but has spread to different parts of the UK.

Restricted code: An idea advanced by Bernstein (and much disputed) that working-class speakers use context-based, limited forms of language.

Tip

In Section A of the Paper 2 exam, it is up to you to select the research that will help you address the question most effectively. You may find that you draw from different areas of diversity and change, not just from a single topic. You must read the question carefully and identify the areas that are most relevant. There is no set way to answer any question: take time to carefully plan the theory you wish to include, then ensure you can use the theory to form a clear debate.

Research on language and identity: Llamas' Middlesbrough study (2000)

Llamas investigated variation and change in the dialect of Middlesbrough (a town in the north-east of England). She examined the variation of the phonemes /p/, /t/, /k/ which could be pronounced as either full plosives (the RP pronunciation), glottalised stops (the RP pronunciation with a slight glottalisation) or as full glottal stops (complete closure of the glottis so no sound occurs).

She found a considerable amount of variation; the age and gender of the speaker were factors that influenced the pronunciation of these phonemes. Females in the study used the glottal stop the most and this goes against commonly held views that glottal stops are used mostly by working-class male speakers.

Llamas found that the younger speakers used the glottalised and glottal variants more than the older speakers, and she believed that younger Middlesbrough speakers may be converging with areas further north in Tyneside. She believed this was linked to the speakers' attitudes towards different parts of the North-East and, importantly, their sense of identity. Llamas concluded that regional identity in Middlesbrough was a fluid concept and the speakers in her study were constructing their identity through variations in the production of the /p/, /t/ and /k/ phonemes. The glottalised stop chosen by younger people expressed their identity with the North-East.

Activity 19

Complete the following tasks on separate paper.

1. Sum up in your own words how the speakers from Middlesbrough were showing their identity.

2. How does your accent link with your identity? Do you find you adapt your language to suit the different identities that you perform? Give at least one example.

3. Llamas describes the glottalised pronunciation of /p/, /t/, /k/ by younger speakers in Middlesbrough as a 'change in progress'. What other research have you studied that demonstrated a change in progress? You could think about the use of vocal fry among women in the US, or the spread of uptalk, for example.

4. Think of any changes that have taken place in language during your lifetime.

Activity 20

Now you have revised the topic of regional variation, on separate paper, describe the difference between non-standard English and informal English. Give your own examples of each. Try to write at least one paragraph.

Ethnicity and language diversity

This chapter builds on many of the ideas you have already looked at about language diversity, such as how language use relates to people's identity and place of origin. An individual's ethnic background will undoubtedly influence how they use and construct language, but the connection between language and ethnicity is more complex than might be expected.

Activity 1

Remind yourself of some of the key terms involved in ethnicity and language diversity by writing a short definition of each of the terms below:

Ethnicity: _____

Race: _____

Ethnolect: _____

Multiethnolect: _____

Links between language and ethnicity are often related to people's sense of heritage and identity. **British Black English** (BBE), for example, is rooted in the English spoken by those who arrived in Britain from the Caribbean from the late 1940s onwards and who spoke varieties of Caribbean English from Jamaica, Barbados and St Lucia. More recently, BBE has adapted to soak up influences from West Africa, while many younger speakers of all ethnicities have moved towards multiethnolects such as Multicultural London English (MLE) and **Multicultural Urban British English** (MUBE).

Activity 2

Think about the different languages spoken by people in the UK from a range of different ethnic backgrounds. Using the diagram overleaf, make a note of the languages other than English that are used by people around you at your school or college and in the wider local community. Do you speak a language or languages other than English? Think about why heritage or family languages are important.

Key terms

British Black English: A wide-ranging label, but often referring to a variety used by some speakers within the Caribbean community in the UK.

Multicultural Urban British English: A label that refers to the way in which Multicultural London English has spread to other large conurbations in the UK.

Other languages spoken in the UK beside English	⟹	

Languages I hear in school or my local community	⟹	

Languages I speak	⟹	

Why are heritage or family languages important?	⟹	

Activity 3

Read back through your textbook and notes to gather your ideas about what MLE and MUBE are and some of their characteristics. On separate paper, respond to the following questions.

• What are some of the recognised phonological and lexical features of MLE?

• Why is it too simplistic to say that MLE is 'Jafaican'?

• In what ways does MLE fit the definition of a multiethnolect and why is it not an ethnolect?

• What is the difference between MLE and MUBE?

Activity 4

Read Extract 1, taken from Wales Online in 2013, which puts forward some claims about MLE and its speakers. The full article can be found at: https://www.walesonline.co.uk/news/wales-news/forget-butty-its-bruv-now-6311555.

Extract 1

> https://www.walesonline.co.uk/news/wales-news/forget-butty-its-bruv-now-6311555.

Forget Butty… it's Bruv now, innit! Behind the new 'Jafaican' dialect on the streets of Wales

Youngsters are dropping their Welsh accents in favour of an Afro-Caribbean/Welsh mish-mash

A new dialect is emerging on the streets of Wales as youngsters ditch their Kairdiff, Newport or Valleys accents for an Afro-Caribbean/Welsh mish-mash.

Some key ideas from each of the commentators mentioned in the text have been summarised below. Read these and then, on separate paper, write a short evaluation of the ideas and opinions being put forward by each person, relating them to your own understanding of the topic.

Goldie Lookin Chain rapper John Rutledge, aka Eggsy: 'everyone is going to end up speaking exactly the same at some point. [...] Lots of rappers do it and that is really weird, because 25 years ago rappers in Britain were putting on American accents. But now they are doing this Jafaican thing. It's funny because what they really want is identity. They don't even know why they are speaking like this but they know it is something to do with a big city.'

Martin Blakebrough, from the Welsh drugs help service Kalaidoscope: 'It is the music they listen to [...] We find that more and more it takes on a lot of Afro-Caribbean language and youngsters follow that. [...] We see words sometimes being used inappropriately.'

'White kids are heard attempting to bond with black teens by calling them, "n****r."'

'If you are part of the white community, it is clearly not appropriate. They feel like it is appropriate to a black person because they share an identity. But that is not the case.'

Linguist Paul Kerswill, who spent eight years studying the development of Multicultural London English: 'They pick up elements, even if they can switch it off when they go home to their parents [...] There is maybe a cool factor in being like a certain group even if you don't come from that background.'

Mercedes Durham, a linguist from Cardiff University: 'All accents are changing in some ways.'

Code-switching and code-mixing

All language users can move between different types of language, shifting from one style to another depending on the context. Speakers of more than one language or variety can also move between the two (or more) forms to express different aspects of their identity at given times.

Activity 5

1. Remind yourself of the definitions of the terms code-switching and code-mixing.

Code-switching: _____

Code-mixing: _____

2. a. Read Extract 2, below, taken from John McWhorter's book *Talking Back, Talking Black*.

b. Identify two key ideas from this extract that could be used with the Paper 2, Section A, Question 1 or 2 stem 'Evaluate the idea that…'. On separate paper, see if you can map out a possible answer to one of them, drawing on your understanding of this area and others.

Extract 2

Just as some are under the impression that someone who speaks Black English cannot speak Standard English too, others might think that a black person who speaks Standard English cannot also be fluent in Black English. More to the point, they assume that when such a person speaks Black English, they're a fake… One does not switch to Black English randomly, however; the dialect is an expression of cultural fellowship among black people.

Polish English speakers

Ethnicity is not simply a question of skin colour but of a sense of identity linked to family history and identity.

Activity 6

Linguist, Rob Drummond carried out work in Manchester in 2012 looking at the ways in which Polish people spoke English. Read Extract 3, opposite, from *Language Diversity and World Englishes* which explains the research. Answer the following questions.

1. What does the research tell us about how some Polish speakers of English produce variants of 'ing' sounds?

_____

_____

_____

2. What is meant by the phrase 'perform their ethnic identity'?

_____

_____

_____

3. How is this area relevant to other aspects of language diversity that you have studied?

_____

_____

_____

_____

_____

_____

_____

_____

_____

_____

Extract 3

…in the course of his research into the pronunciation of 'ing' in words such as 'feeling', 'swimming', and 'living' for example, he found something he wasn't expecting. In addition to the predictable variants of '-ing' [ɪŋ] and '-in' [ɪn] he also found quite a few people using '-inK' [ɪŋk]. This wasn't surprising in itself, as it was clearly a Polish-influenced pronunciation (in Polish, the /ŋ/ sound can only occur before a /k/ or a /g/), but what was surprising was that there was no relationship between the use of this variant and an individual's level of English. In other words, the '-inK' pronunciation wasn't just being used because individual speakers hadn't mastered the local pronunciation, so there must be some other reason.

That reason turned out to be related to people's future plans. One of the questions people were asked related to what they intended to do in the future. Did they plan to stay in the UK or return to Poland? People who intended to return to Poland were more likely to use the '-inK' pronunciation, and less likely to use the '-in' pronunciation (this is the most common non-standard variant among British native English speakers). Because some of these speakers had very good English, Drummond interpreted this finding as an example of individuals using this pronunciation more or less consciously in order to signal some kind of allegiance or **solidarity** with their Polish ethnicity. In other words, they were very likely able to produce a more native-like pronunciation of 'ing', but this was a small way in which they could perform their ethnic identity.

> **Key term**
>
> **Solidarity:** A feeling of connection with others, mutual support.

> **Tip**
>
> As with all the other aspects of language diversity you are revising, there is a great degree of crossover; people's language identities are formed through intersecting aspects of their social backgrounds, the contexts they are communicating in and how they wish to come across to others at a given time. If you appreciate and evaluate this complexity, you can access the higher levels of the mark scheme.

International Englishes

Key term

World Englishes:
Varieties of English that
are used in different
countries around the
world, mainly in areas
that were formerly
colonised, such as
India and Singapore.
These countries have
their own version of
Standard English.

The way that the English language has spread around the world and developed a new life and identity in other countries is an aspect of both language change and language diversity. It could therefore be a relevant area of discussion, as with all the change and diversity areas for both Question 1 and Question 2 in Section A of Paper 2 and in Section B as a focus for language discourses.

As with regional variety in the UK, language change, and social and occupational groups, it is impossible to cover everything concerning the spread of English internationally, but there are some core ideas that are important to understand and a range of case studies and wider resources you could make use of.

Organising your notes

Activity 1

Make sure you do the following before starting to look at the ideas for exam questions at the end of this chapter.

- Look at the ways in which English spread beyond England into other parts of the British Isles. Identify a range of countries around the world where English became an important language and select a few of these to explore in more depth. For each one, identify reasons for English being there, how it grew and the status it had in the past and has now.

- Choose two or three varieties of International Englishes. Copy and complete the following table with one column for each of them. (Leave the final two rows for now – you will need to look in more detail at models of **World Englishes** before you can complete these.)

- Where you are being asked about 'differences' think about these as in relation to UK Standard English.

Variety of International Englishes	1.	2.	3.
Overview (include details such as when English first arrived, native languages present and nature of the status of English in this country)			
Number of speakers			
Where it is spoken			
Phonological differences			
Vocabulary differences			
Grammatical differences			
Orthographical differences			
Other differences			
Position in Kachru's circles			
Position in Schneider's model			

Revising the models

Linguists have proposed different models for explaining and describing the relationships between different varieties of English around the world. As well as understanding how English began a new life in different territories around the world and the nature of the English spoken in these places, it is important to have an overview of these models. They can help provide you with a conceptualised understanding of the different strands: something that is important for a good AO2 mark.

Activity 2

Using the following diagrams, your notes and textbook, complete the tasks on page 104 on separate paper.

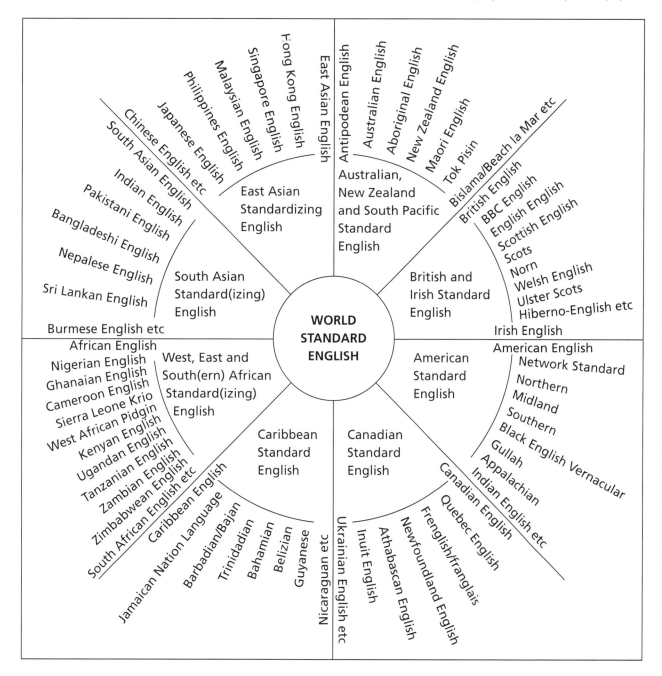

McArthur's circle of World English

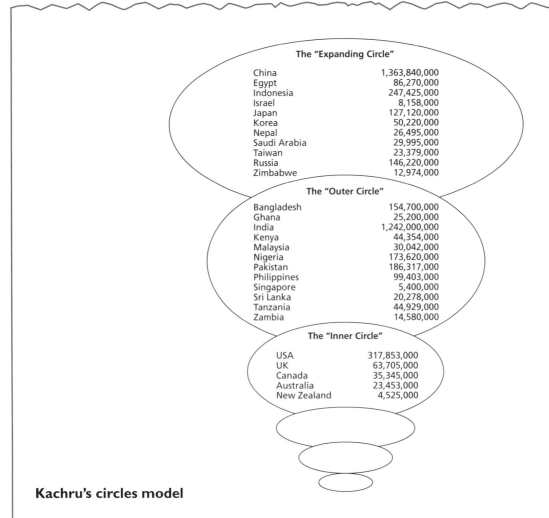

The "Expanding Circle"

China	1,363,840,000
Egypt	86,270,000
Indonesia	247,425,000
Israel	8,158,000
Japan	127,120,000
Korea	50,220,000
Nepal	26,495,000
Saudi Arabia	29,995,000
Taiwan	23,379,000
Russia	146,220,000
Zimbabwe	12,974,000

The "Outer Circle"

Bangladesh	154,700,000
Ghana	25,200,000
India	1,242,000,000
Kenya	44,354,000
Malaysia	30,042,000
Nigeria	173,620,000
Pakistan	186,317,000
Philippines	99,403,000
Singapore	5,400,000
Sri Lanka	20,278,000
Tanzania	44,929,000
Zambia	14,580,000

The "Inner Circle"

USA	317,853,000
UK	63,705,000
Canada	35,345,000
Australia	23,453,000
New Zealand	4,525,000

Kachru's circles model

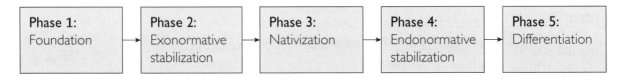

| Phase 1: Foundation | → | Phase 2: Exonormative stabilization | → | Phase 3: Nativization | → | Phase 4: Endonormative stabilization | → | Phase 5: Differentiation |

Schneider's dynamic model

1. Write a short sentence explaining Kachru's ideas about the nature of each of his circles.

2. Write a short paragraph explaining the nature of the relationship between the different circles of Kachru's model. What are the differences between them?

3. Explain why Kachru's circles model is preferred to McArthur's by many linguists.

4. Some have argued that Kachru's model does not account for different speakers' *proficiency* in English within the same country. Can you explain what might be meant by this and why it might be a problem?

5. How useful is Schneider's model in explaining how varieties of International English develop? Write a short paragraph explaining what this model offers that others might not.

6. Now go back to Activity 1 and complete the final two rows of your table.

English as a lingua franca (ELF)

Another key area of recent discussion has been the rise of what some linguists have termed **English as a lingua franca** (ELF). This is not a variety of International English but a form of English that is used as a contact language among speakers who have different first languages. ELF is a practical way of using English in situations and with other speakers where a shared form of communication is required. English happens to be the most common tool for this because (according to Crystal, 2003) of its historical position in the world, its use in academia, its link to the UK and USA as economic and cultural powers and for a number of practical political reasons.

Key term

English as a lingua franca (ELF): The role of English as a bridging language in interactions where it is not everyone's first language.

Activity 3

For each of the reasons below, write a sentence or two explaining why English is the language most commonly used as an ELF, giving examples to illustrate. What other reasons can you think of?

- Historical position: _____

_____

_____

- Academia: _____

_____

_____

- Economic power: _____

_____

_____

- Cultural power: _____

_____

_____

- Practical political reasons: _____

_____

_____

- Internet and technology: _____

_____

_____

Activity 4

ELF is not a geographical variety of English therefore, but a form of English used in certain situations. Jennifer Jenkins and Barbara Seidlhofer (among others) identify a range of different features that are common to ELF in different situations, some of which are included below. Match the technical description on the left to the relevant example on the right.

Technical description
Dropping the third person -s in verbs
Omitting determiners
Phonological substitution
Use of invariant tag questions
Omission of plural endings

Example
She walk/he run
We saw many animal there.
They play well, isn't it?
Pronouncing 'this' as 'dis'
Put package down

Debates about International English

As well as looking at how and why English has spread around the world, it is important to understand the different arguments around the topic and why it is still a contentious area. As with all the other areas of focus for Paper 2, Section A, you could face texts discussing and debating International English in Section B and be asked to write an opinion piece about them, but you might need to address debates and arguments around the topic in Section A as well.

Activity 5

For each of the statements below, on separate paper, make a note of views for and against them, and support with reference to ideas from language study. One has been started for you.

1. 'England has lost control of English.'

Ideas to consider:

* Has England ever truly had 'control' over the language? What is meant by 'control' here?

* If English is being used around the world, what business is that of people in England?

* The linguist Mario Saraceni has argued that the 'umbilical cord' between Britain and English needs to be cut and that ideas about 'ownership' over any language are not helpful.

* Alternatively, it could be argued that people often have very strong feelings about language and that it is linked to identity, so it is unsurprising that some might feel a sense of loss to see and hear English used in ways that are not familiar to them.

2. 'International Englishes are inferior versions of British English.'

3. 'There should be a form of Standard English agreed upon and used by all English speakers around the world.'

Exam-style questions

Activity 6

As explained earlier, the essay questions in Paper 2, Section A take the form of an idea that needs to be evaluated. Have a look at some of the following quotations about International Englishes and extract one or two key ideas from them, then turn them into a question. On separate paper, then plan and write your response to such a question.

1. The writer Lane Greene argues that he 'doesn't see British English – or any other kind of English – being blandly homogenised into one global, and mostly American, variety'.

_____

_____

_____

_____

2. The journalist Matthew Engel claims that, 'We are in danger of subordinating our language to someone else's – and with it large aspects of British life'.

_____

_____

_____

_____

3. The linguist Lynne Murphy argues that 'British people get upset about Americanisms because they are used to thinking of Britain as being the centre of English, and the centre has moved. And so the fact that Americanisms are singled out is indicative that what's going on there is really feelings about loss of power and feeling like American English is taking over what used to be something of theirs'.

_____

_____

_____

_____

_____

Occupation and language diversity

Occupational language can be broadly categorised under the heading of **sociolect**, so you will need to be prepared to answer questions on occupational language in its own right or refer to occupational varieties and/or registers as part of a wider answer on sociolect.

Revising case studies

> ## Activity 1
>
> **1.** One of the most important aspects of your revision for this topic is to make sure you have a good range of examples and case studies to draw upon. Look back through your notes and in your textbook for examples of occupations and the language that they use.
>
> **2.** Try to identify three different occupations and on separate paper, group their language use under the headings below. Remember to think about the written and electronic communication used within the occupational groups as well as their spoken language. An example has been given for each question within the headings.
>
> ### Lexis and semantics
>
> - What field-specific vocabulary and/or jargon is used within this occupation?
>
>   (For example, 'subcutaneous emphysema' – trapped air under the skin – in the medical profession.)
>
> - Are there any words or phrases used that have more common meanings but which are used in a more specialised or **idiomatic** way?
>
>   (For example, 'scope' has different meanings in publishing and the military, while 'out for the count' relates to boxing.)
>
> - Are there any vocabulary items that are deliberately *not* used in this occupational group?
>
>   (For example, references to death are often treated very **euphemistically** in the funeral business – 'laid to rest', 'passed away', 'left us'.)
>
> ### Grammar
>
> - Are there any syntactical structures used within the speech or writing of this occupational group that are different to those of other groups?
>
>   (For example, sports coaching often makes use of more bald directives than other forms of training and teaching, while counsellors might be expected to use more questions.)

- Is there an expectation that Standard or non-standard English be used in the occupation?

  (For example, teaching is expected to make use of Standard English, while a radio DJ might be expected to use some non-standard English.)

Phonology

- Is there an expectation of a particular accent or tone of voice in this occupation?

  (For example, are some more 'trustworthy' or 'authentic' accents used in telesales positions? Is a sympathetic tone more sought after in 'caring' occupations?)

Graphology/orthography

- In written or electronic communication are particular symbols, spellings or aspects of visual design different to other groups?

  (For example, the use of -z rather than -s plurals online: 'lulz', 'the internetz'; or rappers respelling 'dog' as 'dogg' or 'America' as 'Amerikkka'.)

Discourse structure

- Are there expectations of particular structures to interaction in this group?

  (For example, in hierarchical organisations, is there an expectation that topics will be introduced by those in a senior position?)

Functions of language

Think carefully about the different ways in which language is used in some occupations. It is not always as simple as saying that it is used for one main function, because most occupations require a range of different interactions and uses of language on a daily basis.

For example, a sales assistant in a technology shop might need to do some or all of the following:

- talk to other shop workers

- assist customers with queries

- explain how products work or their specifications

- listen to complaints or problems from customers face-to-face or on the phone

- write and respond to emails from managers and other shops

- take part in a staff meeting

- deal with deliveries and returns, talking to drivers and couriers

- deal with sales reps offering products and discounts.

Activity 2

Look at the list of occupations below and, on separate paper, write down all the different functions of language that might be used in them, and examples of the kind of talk or writing this might involve.

- Customer service adviser in a supermarket
- Plumber
- Primary school teacher
- Police officer
- Office manager
- Estate agent

Understanding concepts, research and theory

Key terms

Corpus (plural corpora): A collection of searchable language data stored on a computer.

Discourse community: An alternative term for a community of practice.

Inferential framework: Knowledge built up over time and used in order to understand meanings that are implicit.

Phatic: Language that is devoid of content but that supports social relationships.

Activity 3

Think carefully about some of the linguistic research that has been carried out, and the ideas put forward on occupational language. Look at your notes for the case studies listed below. On separate paper, write a short paragraph on each of them.

- John Swales and **discourse communities**
- Michael Nelson's work with a **corpus** of business language
- Drew and Heritage's work on **inferential frameworks**
- Almut Koester's discussion of **phatic** talk
- Kim and Elder's study of air pilots
- Janet Holmes and the Language in the Workplace project

Activity 4

In the A level exam you are not provided with data as part of your essay question, but one good way to prepare is to think about data as providing you with examples and to ask what data can tell you about the topic. The following question could be used alongside Text A (opposite).

Evaluate the idea that occupational language needs to be in plain English.

Read Text A which is taken from a website that campaigns for plain English in public communication. Answer the questions that follow it.

Text A

1. What aspects of occupational English are raised by the data and how could you write about them?

_____

_____

_____

_____

2. What is 'Plain English' and why is it relevant to a discussion of occupational language?

_____

_____

_____

_____

_____

_____

_____

3. Which other areas of discussion might you bring in from beyond the data?

_____

_____

_____

_____

_____

_____

_____

Links to other areas

Occupational language comes under the broader heading of sociolect.
Understanding how different areas of the course overlap and seeing the interplay
between various aspects of language and identity are essential for hitting the
higher levels of the mark scheme. The next two tasks ask you to consider the
overlap between occupational language and other areas.

Activity 5

Text B is an extract from an interview with a female police officer in the USA. It forms part of a chapter on women working in traditionally all-male occupations by the linguistic anthropologist Bonnie McElhinny. Read the extract and answer these questions.

1. What might this extract tell us about the link between language, occupation and gender?

_____

_____

2. Which theories and models of language study might be applied to the ideas put forward in this interview?

_____

_____

_____

_____

Text B

Interviewer: Do you think women who come on this job start to act in masculine ways?

Officer: Umhm.

Interviewer: Like what are some of the things you see?

Officer: Your language. I know mine, mine changes a lot from… When I'm at work I always feel like I have to be so, so like gruff you know. And normally I'm not like that. I'm usually kinda bitchy but I'm not like real. Sometimes I try to be like such a hard ass. I, I don't smile as much. I'm not saying that men, you know that's a masculine trait. I think you…you have to pick up maybe not necessarily fighting but techniques to subdue people or just hold them or whatever and I don't think that's naturally feminine either you know. I think it's mostly language. You know… My, mine's atrocious sometimes. I've toned it down a lot. When I first started you know cause I worked with a lot of guys it seemed like, they didn't may not even have swore but I felt like I had to almost like be tough or something around them you know. And that was my way of being tough.

Interviewer: Is it like mostly profanity, or do you do it like with tone of voice or something?

Officer: Little bit of both.

> **Stretch**
>
> Record a workplace conversation (or a range of workplace conversations if possible). Transcribe the data and carefully annotate it. Write an analysis of how language is used to construct and perform a workplace identity.

As outlined in the introduction to Paper 2, Section A, the essay questions in this part of the paper give you an idea to evaluate. Language change is a very wide topic and you can't hope to cover everything that has changed between the birth of English and the day of the examination, so it is important to understand the main areas and make sure you have a good overview of some key ideas and principles. It is also important that you have your own case studies and examples to refer to.

What has changed?

English has changed in a number of ways since it first emerged as a language in its own right.

Activity 1

1. Thinking about the different language levels and using your textbook and class notes, copy and complete the table below with at least three changes per language level. Some examples have been filled in to start you off.

Graphology and orthography	I. Spellings have become more regularised since the 18th century because of the growth of Standard English and the use of dictionaries, for example, kwene/queen.
Lexis and semantics	I. New words have come into English having been 'borrowed' from other languages, for example, sushi, karaoke.
Phonology	
Syntax and morphology	
Text and discourse	

2. Choose one example from each row and add specific examples you could use to illustrate this change.

Why has language changed?

It is obvious that English has changed over time but what has driven those changes?

Again, making use of your textbook and class notes, think about what has led to language changing. Complete the table below and make a note of at least three examples of how language has changed as a result of each of the following factors. Some examples have been filled in to start you off.

Technology	1. The invention of the printing press led to the rapid growth of printed materials, helping spread written forms of English around the country.
Migration and movement of people	1. The influence of Caribbean English on different aspects of British English has come about since the 1950s and the arrival of people from the Caribbean in the UK. For example, 'vexed' for 'annoyed' has come back into use and 'bare' for 'many'/'really'.
Social change	
War and conflict	
Education	

Key term

Compounding: Adding two existing words together to create a new word.

How has language changed?

Having thought about what has changed and why these changes have happened, it is also important to make sure you have a clear understanding of some of the processes of language change.

Activity 3

1. Looking at lexical change to begin with, match the word formation process to the examples given below.

Word formation process	Examples
Compounding	fridge, frag
Blending	mic drop, rage-quit
Initialism/**acronym**	smorgasbord, anime
Back-formation	Brexit, manterrupting
Borrowing	FOMO (fear of missing out), RPG (role-playing game)
Clipping	antifascist, preload
Affixation	burgle, edit

2. Now look at Text A, a feature about new words entering the dictionary, on page 117.

a. How would you classify the examples featured into different word formation processes?

_____

_____

b. What are the main patterns that you notice for these new words and which areas of life are they linked to?

_____

_____

_____

Key terms

Acronym: Initials that can be pronounced as words (e.g. SIM).

Blending: Using parts of existing words to form a new word.

Borrowing: Incorporating words and phrases from another language.

Tip

Make sure that you have a range of good examples by following the stories about the Word of the Year (WOTY) for each of the major dictionaries in the UK and beyond. Some suggestions for keeping up to date with these are:

- Oxford Dictionaries: https://en.oxforddictionaries.com/word-of-the-year/word-of-the-year-2017
- Collins Dictionary: https://www.collinsdictionary.com/woty
- Macquarie Dictionary (Australia): https://www.macquariedictionary.com.au/resources/view/word/of/the/year/
- American Dialect Society (Word of the Year awards): https://www.americandialect.org/woty

Text A

After much discussion, debate, and research, the Oxford Dictionaries Word of the Year 2016 is *post-truth* – an adjective defined as 'relating to or denoting circumstances in which objective facts are less influential in shaping public opinion than appeals to emotion and personal belief'.

Which words made the shortlist?

alt-right
(in the US) an ideological grouping associated with extreme conservative or reactionary viewpoints, characterized by a rejection of mainstream politics and by the use of online media to disseminate deliberately controversial content

glass cliff
used with reference to a situation in which a woman or member of a minority group ascends to a leadership position in challenging circumstances where the risk of failure is high

hygge
a quality of cosiness and comfortable conviviality that engenders a feeling of contentment or well-being (regarded as a defining characteristic of Danish culture)

chatbot
a computer program designed to simulate conversation with human users, especially over the Internet

adulting
the practice of behaving in a way characteristic of a responsible adult, especially the accomplishment of mundane but necessary tasks

Brexiteer
a person who is in favour of the United Kingdom withdrawing from the European Union

woke
(US informal) alert to injustice in society, especially racism

coulrophobia
extreme or irrational fear of clowns

Latinx
a person of Latin American origin or descent (used as a gender-neutral or non-binary alternative to Latino or Latina)

Activity 4

1. Meanings also change over time for existing words. Add two examples for each semantic change process.

Semantic change process	Examples
Pejoration	
Amelioration	
Narrowing	
Broadening	
Semantic bleaching	

Key terms

Amelioration: A process whereby a word or phrase develops more positive connotations. For example, 'nice' used to mean ignorant (from the Latin 'nescire' meaning 'to not know').

Broadening: A process by which words acquire a broader reference. For example, 'hoover' can be used as a general label for vacuum cleaners, but it was formerly the name of a particular brand.

Narrowing: A process by which words acquire a narrower reference. For example, 'deer' used to refer to animals in general, not to a specific animal.

Key terms

Metaphor: A language strategy for bringing two unrelated ideas together in order to suggest a new way of looking at something. Metaphors are common where something is difficult to understand because it is complex or abstract, so it is compared with something simpler or more concrete.

Political correctness: A term used, usually by conservative commentators, to object to the idea of consciously changing language because it is considered unfair to different groups.

2. Think carefully about what these semantic changes might tell us about the nature of language change and the link between language and society. On separate paper, write a paragraph of your ideas.

3. There are several ways in which linguists have described how language changes. On separate paper, write a summary in two or three sentences of each of the following models, explaining what they are and how they explain change.

- The wave model
- The s-curve model
- Substratum theory
- Crystal's tide **metaphor**
- Random fluctuation theory
- Functional theory

Language reform

Language reform movements in the late 20th and early 21st centuries have campaigned to change the ways in which people use language. These movements have often claimed that language:

- can be unclear and obfuscatory – they have campaigned to make the language clearer and more accessible to all people (for example, the Plain English Campaign)

- might be viewed as offensive and discriminatory to different social groups and have sought to remove or challenge such language (for example, what has been termed the '**political correctness**' movement)

- can be open to 'reclamation' and have consciously adopted negative words using them in a way that challenges others' perceptions (for example, the 'Slutwalks' movement, or respelling and reclaiming a racially offensive term such as 'nigger').

> **Stretch**
>
> Read Ed Yong's article 'The Randomness of Language evolution' at: https://www.theatlantic.com/science/archive/2017/11/drove-not-drived/544595/.
>
> In this piece, Yong puts forward an alternative way of viewing how language changes. Summarise his key points and then write a short evaluation of these ideas and link them to others you have come across about the nature of language change.

Activity 5

1. How can you use your knowledge of language change to revise this area of the subject? Consider the following exam-style question:

> Evaluate the idea that language change can be controlled and directed.
> **[30 marks]**

Think specifically about language reform movements and on separate paper, answer the following questions.

a. Which language reform movements have attempted to control or direct the language?

b. What examples of language have they tried to change and why?

c. What alternatives have they proposed and why are these seen as more positive?

d. What success have these movements had?

e. What views have linguists and commentators expressed about such movements?

f. What is your own evaluation of language reform movements?

2. Now, read Extracts 1–3, below and on page 120, about language reform and write your own brief summary of each, followed by a short evaluation, drawing on your own study of language. Once you have done this, see if you can integrate their ideas and examples with your answers for questions a–f.

Extract 1: Comedian, Richard Herring

In one of the interviews today I also discussed disablist language, something that I think many comics are guilty of using as convenient and humourless punchlines. I don't think any of them would do the same with the word 'nigger' or 'paki' but they're happy to use 'mong' or 'retard' as a means of getting a laugh. And audiences will laugh at those words too and rarely even complain about them. But I think they do equate with those racial and homophobic epithets that are rarely heard these days. They do confirm the stereotype of disabled people and contribute to their further isolation in a world that already tries to pretend they don't exist.

Extract 2: Daily Mirror, August 2006

AUF WIEDERSEHEN TO PET.. HINNY.. DEAR.. DARLING.. LOVE.. AND SWEETHEART

Council bans staff from using traditional terms of affection

GEORDIES have been told to say auf wiedersehen to the word pet*.

The term of affection has been banned along with hinny, dear and love. Council workers are also not allowed to say darling or sweetheart in a politically correct crackdown.

But Franc Roddam, creator of the hit TV series *Auf Wiedersehen, Pet,* blasted yesterday: 'Once they start interfering with terms of endearment, soon we'll have to have a lawyer present when we make love.'

All Newcastle city council staff are being sent on 'equality and diversity' courses to teach them how to avoid causing offence.

*(*Note: Auf Wiedersehen Pet was the title of a 1980s drama featuring Geordie builders who went to Germany looking for work.)*

Extract 3: Linguist, Deborah Cameron writing on her blog in 2017

I'm always wary of approaches to sexism which treat changing language as a panacea. Language is rarely the root cause of the problem: it's the outward and visible symptom of a deeper cultural disease.

Attitudes to language change

Attitudes to language change can often be classed as descriptive or prescriptive (terms which you have come across already in this book); however, that is sometimes a rather simplistic division to make and you might be advised to interrogate each idea a bit more fully.

Activity 6

Look at the examples of opinions about how the word 'so' is used in conversation. Try to sort them into two groups: one for opinions that you feel are the most critical of language change and one for those which are either neutral or accepting of change. Tick your choice in the table.

Opinions	Critical of change	Neutral / accepting of change
1. 'I have been increasingly irritated over the last couple of years by the increasing use of the word "so" when prefacing a sentence.'		
2. 'I don't think "so" is an appropriate word with which to begin a sentence.'		
3. 'Every time I hear it, the hair on my neck rises and my teeth bare in a grimace.'		
4. 'The misplaced "so" has invaded everyday speech like some noxious weed in an untended garden.'		
5. 'One explanation is that in this case, "so" is being used as a filled pause, much in the way that "well", "um", and "like" are used in conversation.'		
6. '"So" is not being used just to fill a pause, it seems, but as a tool for conversation management.		

Opinions about language are many and varied, and can be expressed in a range of ways. Part of your work in Section B, Question 3, is to explore the ways in which language discourses are produced and replicated, but there is also crossover with this in Section A if you are asked, or choose, to discuss attitudes to language change.

Activity 7

1. Jean Aitchison's metaphors for prescriptive attitudes towards language are well known and can be a useful way of describing and characterising different strands of prescriptivism. Remind yourself of her three metaphors by writing a short definition for each:

Crumbling castle: _____

Damp spoon: _____

Infectious disease: _____

2. Other models can also be helpful. Robert Lane Greene's ideas of declinism and sticklerism are useful ways of describing similar prescriptive attitudes. Write a short definition for each of these too:

Declinism: _____

Sticklerism: _____

3. Look at the short quotations about language below and see which of the Aitchison and Greene models might be applied. Are there any other metaphors that could be applied here to describe the attitudes expressed? Annotate the quotations with your ideas. Some clues have been emboldened in the first quotation to get you started.

a. 'The English language is an incredibly rich inheritance. Yet it is being **squandered** by so many young people of all races and backgrounds. Across London and other cities it is increasingly fashionable for them to speak in an **inarticulate** slang full of **vacuous** words such as "innit" and **wilful distortions** like "arks" for "ask" or **tedious** double negatives.

b. 'Actually, I know all about the get-go or, worse still, the git-go. It's an ugly Americanism, meaning "from the start" or "from the off". It adds nothing to Britain's language but it's here now, like the grey squirrel, destined to drive out native species and ravage the linguistic ecosystem.'

c. 'Meanwhile, the most improbable areas of activity are terminally infected. Take the law. Ask any lawyer and they will explain: witnesses in British courts do not testify, they give evidence; nor do they "take the stand" to do this, they go into the witness box. They do things the American way in media reports of court cases, though — day after day.'

Historical change

Having a clear overview of the history of English is an important part of understanding the nature of language change, so it is a good idea to look at sources that offer you an explanation of the different historical periods of the language.

Activity 8

1. Using your textbook, class notes and other sources, on separate paper, write a short set of bullet points for each of the main periods in English language history explaining when these periods were and some of the key developments that took place in each.

2. Try to find at least two texts for each period and think about how you can relate the language used in these texts to the developments across the different language levels that you looked at earlier in this chapter.

   • Old English (Anglo-Saxon), 5th century

   • Middle English, 11th century

   • Early Modern English, 15th century

   • Late Modern English, 18th century

   • Present-day English, 20th century–present

Stretch

Think about what the historical changes listed in Activity 8 might suggest about future developments in English. Read Dominic Watt and Brendan Gunn's 'The Sound of 2066' report which can be found at: http://www.about.hsbc.co.uk/~/media/uk/en/news-and-media/160929-voice-biometrics-sounds-of-britain-2066.pdf.

Write a short summary of their key observations and evaluate this in the light of your knowledge about language change and diversity.

We will now look at some Paper 2, Section A exam-style questions. There are many ways to approach Questions 1 and 2, and no matter what the questions are, there is no set of predetermined points that you would be expected to make. While the way you approach Section A very much depends on the type of questions you are presented with, here is one possible way to work through your essay.

1. Carefully read the two questions and choose which one you want to answer.

2. Read your chosen question again and highlight the key words, ensuring you can define them.

3. Identify which areas the question is addressing.

4. Identify the argument that is being put forward.

5. Identify the counter-argument that could be presented.

6. Which theories and concepts could be related to this argument, either to support or to reject the idea put forward in the question? Can you bring in any other ideas from your class work, research and wider reading?

7. Evaluate the competing arguments and challenge different ideas. What examples can you use to back up the arguments?

It is important that you do the following things in your Paper 2, Section A essay.

1. Construct an argument in an academic style, using an appropriate linguistic register (AO1).

2. Write clearly and organise your answer, guiding your reader (AO1).

3. Refer to a range of language theories and concepts (AO2).

4. Evaluate the ideas you put forward (AO2).

5. Weigh up the argument, show different angles to show understanding of different ideas (AO1/AO2).

What do the levels mean?

AO2 is the main Assessment Objective for Section A questions and it is relatively simple to understand the different levels applied by examiners here.

- Level 1 suggests you have a very limited knowledge of material relevant to the question.

- Level 2 is heading in the right direction but without the detail and precision examiners want to see at higher levels. You might have some familiarity with relevant ideas but not know exactly what to do with them.

- Level 3 is where you show detailed knowledge and understanding, using clear examples to illustrate your argument.

 Tip

Spend 40 to 45 minutes on this question. It is worth 30 marks – the rest of the paper is worth 70 marks so it is important you don't go over time.

- Level 4 builds on Level 3 but also requires you to show detailed knowledge of different ideas and interpretations, along with a sense of the competing arguments.

- Level 5 does all this and adds a sense of overview and conceptualisation of the bigger picture, an evaluation of the competing ideas and perhaps a sense of challenge to the terms of the question itself.

Dealing with the idea in the question

Questions 1 and 2 will each present you with an idea to evaluate. What does the idea relate to? What have you studied that is relevant to the idea? There will be many different ways to approach these ideas and there is no one right way to answer a question like this. However, you need to be able to understand the idea, grasp its scope, choose your areas for discussion and have ideas of your own to relate to, or even challenge, it.

Activity 1

Look at the following ideas and, relate them to areas you have studied as part of your work for Paper 2. Which areas could you cover? Which examples could you bring in and what kind of knowledge do you have about these ideas?

On separate paper, evaluate the following ideas:

- the social groups people belong to completely determine the way they use language

- the ways in which women and men use language are more similar than different

- language change can be controlled and directed

- technology is the main force behind language change.

Evaluating the idea

Tip

You can give your personal view but remain cautious and open-minded when you do so. It is better to tentatively argue, for example, using phrases such as 'it could be said that', 'there seems to be' and 'an alternative view is'.

What does 'evaluate' mean? It means assessing the worth or value of something. All evaluation will need to involve looking at things from different angles and seeing arguments from different sides. Evaluation will also involve making a decision about these different views and putting forward your own argument. In practice, this will involve looking at different arguments, examples and models around language and arguing a case for your viewpoint, drawing on supporting evidence.

As part of your revision for Paper 2, Section A, you should critically evaluate the ideas from language study that you have covered. Your job is to put the research forward to the examiner and then use it to argue. Level 5 for AO2 requires you to 'evaluate and challenge views, approaches and interpretations of linguistic issues'.

Activity 2

Many issues in the methodologies or approaches to research could be challenged. On separate paper, create a table to examine the issues listed below. Make notes beside each issue. Try and add some of your own issues at the bottom of your table.

- Older research is not always very representative. For example, many studies into gender and interaction in the past largely relied on middle-class white American women as their participants.

- Some researchers have based their findings on anecdotal evidence or their own assumptions rather than actual empirical evidence.

- Some researchers have assumed from the outset that there are language differences in the groups they are studying and then set out to prove these differences.

- Some researchers have very small sample sizes and then make generalisations about language.

- Some researchers only examine speakers in one specific context and then make generalisations about how groups of people use language.

- Some researchers presume that all members of particular groups are the same.

- Some researchers assume that it is always men who have power in society and that power itself is shown through particular forms of language.

- One of the limitations of older studies was the technology (or lack of technology) that was available at the time.

Selecting from your knowledge

Some of the questions you are set might focus you quite narrowly on one area of language study, setting out a limited area for you to respond to. Others might be very broad and leave it up to you to select what you think might be the most appropriate areas of discussion.

In most cases, you will have far too many ideas to cram into one essay, so the key task will be to select the most appropriate ideas from that larger list. Think carefully about different arguments. Choose areas that you feel you have a clear understanding of and that you can provide plenty of examples to illustrate. But above all, make sure you have a coherent argument that you can construct from the raw materials.

Think carefully about what you are going to write and what you are going to argue before you put pen to paper. Once you have a plan, consider how to open your response. One suggestion is to start by defining the key words in the question in your introduction and to explain how you will approach them.

Activity 3

Consider the following exam-style question:

> Evaluate the idea that some accents and dialects are viewed less favourably than others.
>
> **[30 marks]**

1. Use a separate sheet to create a mind map of some of your own ideas. A few questions and ideas have been offered to get you started:

- Define the terms (accents and dialects); you could give an example of a regional variety and put forward a few features of that variety.

- Is the idea in the question true? What examples and evidence can you think of to support it?

- Why might this be the case? Think about prescriptivism and its influence on judgements about language.

- Is there an alternative (descriptivist) view?

2. Now write up your essay. Use your mind map to help you. Spend 45 minutes writing and remember to include plenty of reference to language concepts and theory throughout. Weigh up the research, showing an understanding of the argument and the counter-argument. You must show a clear sense of debate in your Section A essay.

Using your knowledge

The mark scheme for AO2 for Questions 1 and 2 requires you to show your knowledge of language change and/or language diversity, but at the higher levels you need to do more than just show what you know. Think carefully about the different arguments around the central idea you have been given and map these out. If you weigh up and evaluate these ideas, you will be able to construct a response that offers a clear line of argument and allows you to develop an overview of the topic.

Activity 4

For each of the ideas below, on separate paper, draw up a planning grid to think of different arguments for and against it. Where possible, make a note of a relevant study, example or theoretical model that you can refer to. Once you have thought of a few, try to number them in the order you might deal with them in an essay.

Ideas

- Language change is driven mostly by social change.

- There are more similarities than differences in the ways that women and men use language.

- The English language is changing and breaking up into many different Englishes.

An example of a planning grid is given here for another idea.

'Evaluate the idea that the social groups people belong to completely determine the way they use language.'	
For	**Against**
We all belong to different social groups – people we spend time with, work with and feel close to – so it is normal to be influenced by the language used in such groups and to use language in similar ways to other members of these groups.	We use language in different ways within different social groups that we are part of. We have choices over language use, so the groups we belong to do not *completely determine* our language.
People within particular discourse communities or communities of practice are engaged in language practices around shared activities. These will inevitably shape language use in similar ways.	While shared activities might shape our language, they do not completely determine it: many different aspects of our identities filter into how we use language. Even within these groups, gender, ethnicity, age and sexuality might all have a different impact on our language use.
Members of groups often use language to do more than communicate ideas but also to communicate identity and belonging. The sense of belonging can be expressed very strongly through language in these groups.	We use varied and multi-faceted functions of language in all walks of life, not just social groups. To claim that belonging to a social group is the main influence is to ignore other important factors.

Starting to write

Before you put pen to paper and start writing your response, you should have a clear plan. Above all, you should know where your argument is going and where you think it will end. Once you have done this, think about writing your introduction.

Activity 5

1. The two responses below are taken from different students' opening paragraphs to this exam-style question:

> Evaluate the idea that language change can be controlled and directed.
> **[30 marks]**

Look at the two examples and make a note of the strengths and weaknesses of each opening.

Student A

Language will always change and there is nothing anyone can do to stop it. Prescriptivists argue that language should not change because it should stay the same but descriptivists say that change is good and can't be stopped. In this essay I will look at these arguments and discuss how language can't be controlled.

Strengths: _____

_____

_____

Weaknesses: _____

_____

_____

Student B

Language changes all the time and has done since English came to be in the 5th century AD. The English used by the Anglo-Saxons is clearly very different to what we speak now in present-day English, not just in terms of its vocabulary but also its sounds and grammar. Some people have tried to control this change but they have mostly been unsuccessful and this is because language generally changes to suit the needs of its users. Others have tried to regulate language and send it in different directions, and some of these attempts have been a little more successful.

Strengths: _____

_____

_____

Weaknesses: _____

_____

_____

2. Now, go back to the three ideas in Activity 4 and write your own introduction for each one. Are your introductions making use of the same strengths and avoiding the weaknesses of the student extracts on pages 126 and 127?

Tip

Your understanding of AO2 is also very important in Question 4 in Section B of Paper 2, where you are asked to 'assess the ideas and issues raised' in the two texts you analyse for Question 3. Your knowledge of relevant ideas from language study can help you secure a much stronger mark for AO2 than if you just stick to the material in the two texts.

While some Paper 2, Section A questions may direct you towards a particular topic area, such as language and gender, other questions may allow more scope, encouraging a more holistic approach and allowing you to draw knowledge from a range of areas. For example, the question on social groups allows you to select information from any of the diversity areas, and the question on language and social change does not specify exactly what is meant by social change, leaving it open to you to explore. It is up to you to decide on the material to select and the information that allows you to best address the question. It is impossible to cover everything, so be selective. Planning time is essential.

Stretch

Go back over the areas you've studied and revised in this section and try and group together ideas according to:

- research that links with language and identity

- research that links with the language of social groups

- any potential overlaps between language change and diversity.

Question 3 in Paper 2, Section B is a demanding task which requires a range of skills. For revision, there are several things that can really help you with this task:

- revise the language levels and make sure you understand how to analyse texts

- think about different language discourses that you have studied across the areas of change and diversity

- practise writing about two texts together and developing a structure to approach this in the exam.

In this chapter, we will start by looking at how you might analyse one text before thinking about dealing with two texts together. But before that, think carefully about what is meant by 'language discourses'.

Language discourses

A key point to understand is that *both* texts will be about language and that makes this task different to the one you will face in Paper 1 where the topic could be anything. The questions in Section B of Paper 2 come under the heading of 'language discourses'. Discourses – for the purposes of this part of the paper – are ways of thinking about, talking about, describing and representing language that put forward a particular way of seeing change and diversity in language.

For example, in this tweet advertising a Radio 4 programme about American English, an assumption is made that 'Americanisms' are annoying and disliked by the British public by using the verb 'wince'.

Radio 4 tweet

Such a view of American English is perhaps part of a wider discourse around certain forms of language being viewed as better or worse, and around language use irritating or upsetting people.

Remind yourself of some of the key discourses around language.

Activity 1

Match the types of discourse to the correct examples. One has been completed for you.

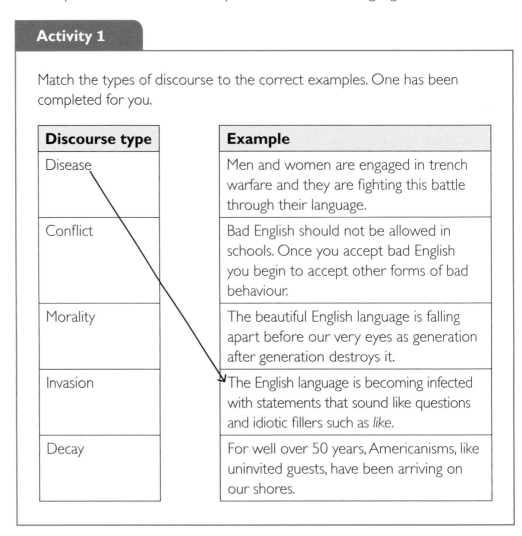

Discourse type	Example
Disease	Men and women are engaged in trench warfare and they are fighting this battle through their language.
Conflict	Bad English should not be allowed in schools. Once you accept bad English you begin to accept other forms of bad behaviour.
Morality	The beautiful English language is falling apart before our very eyes as generation after generation destroys it.
Invasion	The English language is becoming infected with statements that sound like questions and idiotic fillers such as *like*.
Decay	For well over 50 years, Americanisms, like uninvited guests, have been arriving on our shores.

There is not an exhaustive list of language discourses but some of those in Activity 1 are quite common. A good way to revise this area of the course is to explore for yourself the different metaphors and analogies used to describe language, its use and the users of it. From that, you can build up your own understanding of different language discourses and how they are used. Evaluate what these discourses do to language; they all represent language in different ways and sometimes as something else.

A good starting point is to find stories about language on Twitter by following an account such as @EngLangBlog.

Reading for meaning

As explained earlier, you need to have a clear sense of what is being discussed and the views being offered in each text before leaping in to analyse the language. In a moment you will look at an approach to whole texts, but before that, consider these shorter extracts.

Activity 2

Read Extracts 1 and 2 and answer the questions that follow them.

Extract 1 is taken from the opening paragraph of an article about a new app that helps women edit their language choices in emails.

Extract 1

Tami Reiss has a New Year's resolution, and Gmail will help her keep it. With her company's new Chrome browser extension, Reiss has put a bull's-eye on the tempering words and phrases – just, I think, sorry – that clutter up her emails, undermine her authority, and dilute her leadership capacity. Before midnight on New Year's Eve, Reiss wants to get 10,000 other women to pledge to ban these words from their emails, too.

1. Which areas of study around change and diversity is Extract 1 relevant to?

_____

_____

_____

2. What views about women's language might this opening section of the article relate to?

_____

_____

_____

3. List other examples of articles like this which focus on women's language in this way.

_____

_____

_____

Extract 2 is taken from an article in *The Daily Express* about a new report into what English might look and sound like in the future.

Extract 2

Queen's English is being wiped out from London due to the high levels of immigration over the past 50 years. Linguists are predicting the 'th' sound will be obliterated from the capital by 2066 due to the high number of foreigners who cannot pronounce interdental consonants – the name of the sound made by pushing the tongue against the upper teeth.

Multicultural London English – a mixture of Caribbean, West African and Asian accents – is already wiping out indigenous cockney and South East accents.

4. Which areas of study around change and diversity is Extract 2 relevant to?

_____

_____

_____

5. Which discourses about language are being used here?

_____

_____

_____

6. List other examples of articles like this which focus on a similar change in language or that put forward similar views.

_____

_____

_____

Approaching the texts

Once you have read the text and understood the key opinions being put forward (there may be more than one view offered and more than one contributor or writer in each text), you will need to think about the ways in which language is being used to present these ideas.

Many of the skills of textual analysis you will need are the same as those for Paper 1 Section A. The hotspots approach can be used effectively here too, but you also need to think very carefully about *what* is being said about language, *how* an argument is constructed by the producer of each text and *how effectively* those ideas are presented. You must consider the context to the texts and the views they argue. Are these views part of a wider debate about language? Can they be categorised into particular positions?

Connections between the texts

For AO4 you need to show the examiner you can 'make connections across texts'. You must ensure you draw from a range of connections and not just, for example, those based on simple generic features such as audience and purpose. While these may be useful to briefly discuss, they don't enable you to fully engage with meanings and representations – simply comparing very basic content and contextual factors will leave you in Level 2. When you also make relevant and useful connections regarding the language used in the texts, this is Level 3 work. To move up to Level 4 you must also explore how more complex contextual factors could be linked, for example, making connections about how the texts use and produce discourses about language. Level 5 involves an evaluation and critical overview of these connections.

You can use the connections section of the analytical template below and on page 134 to help you compare pairs of texts. You can use this template to help you with each of the paired texts in this section but in your write-up, you should select the most fruitful points of comparison and this will depend on the texts in front of you. For example, if the writers position themselves very differently, as they do in some of the texts in this section, there may be lots to say about this. Sometimes the attitudes towards the topic will be put forward very differently in the two texts, but other times, you may be given texts that contain similar attitudes. It is therefore essential that you have a good overview of the texts and that you select the most useful areas for comparison.

Text A analysis

Content

1. What is the language topic under discussion? How does it relate to topic areas you have studied?

2. What are the key points made?

3. What opinions and views are put forward about the topic?

4. Are the attitudes part of a wider discourse about language?

Context

1. What is the audience, purpose and register of the text?

2. What is the role and status of the writer and how does the writer present himself or herself?

3. How has the writer positioned the reader and how is the reader addressed?

4. Where would this text appear? How would you describe its mode, genre and textual design?

Language

1. How is language being used to represent the language topic?

2. How is language being used to position the writer?

3. How is language being used to address and engage the reader?

Text B analysis

Content

1. What is the language topic under discussion? How does it relate to topic areas you have studied?

2. What are the key points made?

3. What opinions and views are put forward about the topic?

4. Are the attitudes part of a wider discourse about language?

Context

1. What is the audience, purpose and register of the text?

2. What is the role and status of the writer and how does the writer present himself or herself?

3. How has the writer positioned the reader and how is the reader addressed?

4. Where would this text appear? How would you describe its mode, genre and textual design?

Language

1. How is language being used to represent the language topic?

2. How is language being used to position the writer?

3. How is language being used to address and engage the reader?

Comparing Texts A and B

Connections: similarities and differences

a. Is the topic being represented differently in each text?

b. Are the text producers taking different stances?

c. Are similar or different discourses being used?

d. Are they similar or different types of text?

e. Are the contexts for the texts similar or different?

Revising analytical techniques

Over the pages of this chapter you will be given a range of different texts. These texts will be in pairs, each pair on the same topic, just like in the exam. Each pair of texts can be treated as an exam-style question, so if you like you can work from scratch on them and write a full response. The analytical template on pages 133–134 can be used with each pair of texts as a good starting point for your work. Additionally, as you work your way through this chapter, you will be given activities to do on each pair of texts that highlight a particular aspect of discourse analysis. Each of these activities could equally be applied to any of the other pairs of texts, so once you get to the end of the chapter you will have a full toolkit to help you deal with any kind of text.

Paired texts 1

Read Texts A and B. Text A is from *The Guardian* online and was published in November 2013; Text B is an article from the website of *tmrw* magazine in 2018.

Text A

Black Country dialect: no more waggin' for Halesowen pupils

....

A school in Halesowen has banned pupils from using 'woz' and 'it wor me' in the classroom, but the playful local dialect is full of linguistic gems

Comments **502**

Stuart Jeffries

First published on Sunday
17 November 2013 19.30 GMT

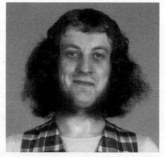

Noddy Holder of Slade in 1974 ... writer of 'Yam-Yammy' hits such as Gudbuy T'Jane.

The Black Country dialect is very different from Birmingham's. Pretend, for a moment, that you care. That's why Brummies call people like me (born in Wolverhampton, raised in Sedgley, although later schooled in Solihull, and suffering a Proustian rush every time I think about the nocturnal vista of flaming blast furnaces I saw when I sat on my nan's back step in Wednesbury) Yam Yams. We're so called because even – imagine! – Brummies think we can't speak proper. 'Yam Yams' is a reference to the Black Country use of 'Yow am' (or yow' m).

This matters because a primary school in Halesowen has banned pupils from using 'gonna', 'woz', 'it wor me' and other purportedly yam-yammy locutions in the classroom in order to improve their grasp of Standard English and, thereby, employability. Dudley North MP (and Yam Yam) Ian Austin backs the ban.

But there's more to Black Country dialect than these words, more even than Walsall-born Noddy Holder's orthographically challenged titles for Yam-Yammy Slade songs (Gudbuy T'Jane, Cum on Feel the Noize). There is a rich linguistic heritage that the Scottish novelist AL Kennedy identified, when I interviewed her about her book *Day*, which tells the story of an eponymous Lancaster bomber tail gunner who hailed from Wednesbury. 'There's an enormous sense of humour in the way Black Country people speak,' said Kennedy. 'It's a very playful and very old language.'

It is both of those things: 'Ow bist' (How are you?), for example, is a contraction of the Middle English 'How be-est thou', to which a reply might be 'Bay too bah', which, like the French *comme ci, comme ça*, means 'I'm not too bad'. 'Bay' means 'am not' (as in 'I bay gooin' ter tell yow agen'). 'Yam Yams' say 'aks' instead of 'ask', 'lickle' not 'little', and when we play roughly we say we are 'lungeous'. 'I ay sid 'er' means 'I haven't seen her'.

I remember my primary school teacher (who came from Lincolnshire) asking his class at Alder Coppice school in Sedgley what we meant by 'saft'. It was, we told him, a gently reproving combination of silly and daft. But we probably didn't put it quite like that.

Later my O-level history teacher Mr England insisted that Black Country dialect, unlike its upstart local rival, Brummie, was more closely related to Middle English than any other regional dialect. That thought is picked up on the superb Sedgley Manor website, which gives a dictionary featuring such gems as 'bunny-fire' (bonfire), 'clack' (eg 'Stop your clack!' ie 'Shut up!'), 'kaylied' (drunk), 'waggin' (bunking off school) and 'lezzer' (not what you're thinking, but a meadow — derived from the Old English 'leasowe'). If you stood in Sedgley Bull Ring now, what you'd hear spoken is a dialect nearer to Chaucerian English than any in use in England.

I'm also moved to tears as I write these words, recalling words that filled my childhood that I'll never speak again. I've been deracinated, standardised, made — linguistically at least — just that little bit less charming.

That fate awaits, perhaps, the pupils of Colley Lane school too. Doubtless they will gain in terms of employability and job security as their headteacher and MP hope, but they risk losing a cherishable and irreplaceable heritage as well.

Text B

https://tmrwmagazine.com/accentism-birmingham/

accentism is a real thing – just ask us brummies

Greg Woodin Feb 21, 2018 In Opinion

it's difficult having a birmingham accent.

It's hard speaking in a way that everyone in the UK detests and continually take the micky out of. When you're told over and over again that your accent is ugly, it's difficult not to feel insecure. It'd be nice to feel pride in the way I speak, at least enough so it doesn't feel good when someone tells me, 'I don't think your accent is that strong'. I'm sick of seeing memes about how the Birmingham accent is the aural equivalent of a kick in the balls, or the world's worst roast dinner. I'm sick of Jeremy Clarkson telling me I sound thick.

In our proudly egalitarian society, it's okay to discriminate against people based on the way they speak. Dr Alexander Baratta from the University of Manchester has called this 'accentism', and has likened it to racism. Baratta reports that people often feel as if they have to flatten out their accents to escape judgment and progress in their careers, but simultaneously feel ashamed at this betrayal of their self-identity. As a Brummie, I can relate to this – and painfully so. I want to be proud of my Brummie roots, but I feel like I have to tone down my twang to be taken seriously. It's got to the point where most of us native Brummies can't even stand the sound of our own voices anymore.

It doesn't help when even academic research seems determined to prove that the Birmingham accent is the ugliest, least intelligent-sounding, least attractive accent in the UK. How many more of these studies must we conduct before we're satisfied that Brummie is the most repulsive sound in the known universe? Recently I came across an article in *The Telegraph*, gleefully reporting a study demonstrating that speaking with a Birmingham accent is 'worse than staying silent'. What's next? How else can we shame Brummies? The ostensible purpose of such research is to find out about people's accent preferences, but the more studies that pile up proving the same point, the more they actually reinforce the preferences they report.

And while I don't doubt that many people genuinely hate how the Birmingham accent sounds, the extent to which our accent preferences are shaped by social norms should not be underemphasised. In my second year of university, I recall speaking to an international student who casually remarked that 'the Birmingham accent is horrible'. Clearly, she couldn't have been too familiar with the accent or she would have noticed that I spoke with it. I wasn't offended. Rather, I interpreted her faux pas as an attempt to align herself with a belief she assumed I also held. In the UK, Brummie is the accent we love to hate – it's how we're supposed to feel. In other parts of the world, people overwhelmingly love the Birmingham accent. This is a decidedly stark contrast, one that I doubt can be put down solely to aesthetic preference.

Things are looking up, though, I guess. Despite a few suspect accents (Helen McCrory, I'm looking at you), Peaky Blinders is doing its best to make the Birmingham accent seem cool. Cillian Murphy in particular does a commendable job with his understated Brummie inflection – and it's certainly an improvement on that horrendous Hotels4u advert a few years ago ('anything for yow, cupcake'), which featured a Birmingham-born actor hamming it up for comedic effect. But, it's unlikely that Peaky Blinders will be enough on its own to shift the public's perception of our accent: it'll take more than a single TV programme to change such a deeply embedded belief.

We self-hating Brummies, we're stuck between a rock and a hard place. We long to leave behind our Brummie roots, but we cringe at the thought of adopting a voice other than our own. All we can do is cross our fingers and hope the tell-tale rise and fall of our voices slowly dissipates over time, so the betrayal feels completely natural. We shouldn't have to feel like this, but it's difficult to foster any kind of pride in our accents when everyone – even academia – keeps telling us how disgusting we sound. As a society, we need to recognise the effects that accentism can have on people and the insecurities it creates. It's no joke.

Tip

Remember that the Assessment Objectives being applied in this question are AO1, AO3 and AO4. There are no AO2 marks to be awarded so you should avoid writing about theory and language research – this is relevant for Questions 1, 2 and 4 of Paper 2.

Activity 3

On separate paper, copy and complete the analytical template on pages 133–134. Once you have done as much as you can, carry out the tasks below.

1. Referring to Text A, complete the second column of the table below by finding an appropriate quotation to support the points made about meaning and representation.

2. Complete the third column to analyse the quotation linguistically.

3. Use paper to continue this table. Identify other points about meaning and representation, find relevant quotations and conduct a precise linguistic analysis.

4. Do the same for Text B by finding quotations that can be analysed and interpreted in a similar way to those in Text A.

Point about meaning and representation	Quotation	Linguistic analysis
The writer represents his extremely negative attitudes to the decision by a local school to ban the use of non-standard dialect words and phrases. This fits into wider discourses about attitudes to non-standard dialects but rather than criticise, as many discourses of this kind do, the writer seeks to defend, support and promote the use of this non-standard dialect.		
The writer positions himself as a proud speaker of the Black Country dialect and throughout the article he defends the use of non-standard dialect forms, with a particular focus on what he refers to as 'Yam Yam' or the Black Country dialect.		

At times, the writer adopts a very tongue-in-cheek approach and he creates humour in order to appeal to the reader and ultimately to convince them of the value and legitimacy of the Black Country dialect.		
The writer represents his own sense of pride and takes a nostalgic approach when looking back at fond memories of the language he used in his childhood.		
The writer attempts to raise the prestige of the Black Country dialect by directly comparing a non-standard dialect form with a well-known French phrase.		

Tip

It's important that you read the texts carefully for meaning. If you don't fully understand the texts the first time then read them again. Misinterpreting the attitudes of the writers or the ideas being put forward will mean you can't access the higher levels for AO3 and AO4.

Stretch

Choose three news articles from a broadsheet newspaper such as *The Guardian* or online sources such as *The Huffington Post* and practise reading them for meaning. Give yourself five minutes to read each article and to extract the most useful points. Write a two-line summary of what the article is about and then think about *how* the writer communicates meanings and representations through the language used. This is good practice for both Paper 2, Section B and Paper 1, Section A.

Stretch

It is always good practice to write your answers in essay form. Write a full analysis of Text A, using the notes from the table. While Question 3 is always a comparison question, writing an analysis of a single text is still useful as you will develop your textual analysis skills. It is also very useful practice for Paper 1 Section A.

Paired texts 2

Read Texts C and D. Text C is a piece from the American website *Jezebel*. Text D is from the British magazine *Good Housekeeping*.

Text C

Google Exec: Women, Stop Saying 'Just' So Much, You Sound Like Children

Tracy Moore

Just when you finally got a handle on saying 'sorry' so much, turns out there's another detrimental phrase in your lexicon keeping you from being taken seriously as a woman: 'Just.' As in, 'Just checking in,' and 'Just following up,' and 'Just wondering if you'd decided.' A former Google exec says this 'permission' word is undermining your authority, and you need to cut down on your 'J Count' pronto.

Writing at *Business Insider,* a former exec at Google and Apple named Ellen Petry Leanse says that, a few years ago, she started noticing that the many women she worked with were using 'just' a lot in emails, conversations, and presentations. Leanse writes:

> It hit me that there was something about the word I didn't like. It was a 'permission' word, in a way — a warm-up to a request, an apology for interrupting, a shy knock on a door before asking 'Can I get something I need from you?'

> The more I thought about it, the more I realized that it was a 'child' word, to riff Transactional Analysis. As such it put the conversation partner into the 'parent' position, granting them more authority and control. And that 'just' didn't make sense.

Well, it *does* make sense if you think about how women are culturally conditioned to be so sympathetic and empathic to the needs of others well before their own that they essentially walk on permanent eggshells, as if invisibly bumping into humanity at all times. It makes plenty of sense when you think about how women live with the ever-present background fear of being perceived as a bitch or a nag, so the only way to prove we are, in fact, correctly socialized to understand that we are nothing special, innately kind-hearted, and also chill as fuck is by apologizing for every possible thing we might ever do, want, think, ask, need, feel. *Sorry you bumped into me! Sorry I had a feeling and expressed it! Sorry I need you to treat me like a person! Sorry for existing at all!*

Once you start paying attention to your own use of hedge words like 'just' and 'sorry,' it is indeed strange to acknowledge how often you work them into sentences and how habitual it can be. I reflexively apologize still when someone bumps into me, not because I assume I was in the wrong, but because I'm not omniscient and maybe I was being oblivious and sorry covers that regardless. I don't even think of it as deferential, I think of it is *being nice*. Because in a perfect world, the other person would say sorry also as a mutual covering of the same potentially egregious ground. If a woman, she usually says sorry back. But if it's a dude, I get a sorry as often as I am given a free monthly supply of tampons (once).

It's not a huge deal, is it? But language shapes consciousness, and if women are the only ones softening their language or self sabotaging their own credibility—even inadvertently, only to be 'nice'—it's still reinforcing that it's a woman trait to be nice.

Women can change a certain amount about female self-presentation if we eliminate hedge words that undermine our authority—Mohr insists that when junior women removed the qualifiers she listed from their communication, they got 'quicker and more substantive responses' in return. That's great. But that may not always be the case. For every story of a qualifier-free move forward, there are a dozen anecdotes of a woman who never had used them in the first place, who always acted like she belonged exactly where she was and knew of what she spoke—and who never stopped catching hell for it.

So yes, take 'just' out of your vocabulary, and don't apologize for it. But don't be surprised, either, if there's just a lot more sorry waiting in line.

Text D

'Can I just say...'

If we qualify a sentence with just, we're essentially asking for permission, says Women's Hour guest presenter Emma Barnett

The other day I read an email that took my breath away. A male friend showed me the resignation message he'd fired off to his boss. Aghast as I am, I'd like to share it with you. It read: 'As discussed on the phone, please accept this email as notice of my resignation. It's become clear to me that I'm not progressing with the speed I had hoped and I'm more in danger of living the same year twice rather than gaining another year of experience. Thank you for your support.'

That's it? I thought. Had he really been so brazen as to send something so pointed, so unapologetic? He hadn't used a single qualifying word. Not even my personal favourite, just: guaranteed to make the most hostile of messages seem friendlier.

Then I realised why his email had so affected me – I was in awe. I couldn't recall ever penning such a blunt message to a colleague. My friend's frankness was a window into the way a whole other group of people converse at work: men.

Just. Actually. Only. All language devices women routinely trot out to soften their requests and ask for permission. An article by former Google executive Ellen Petry Leanse went viral last year when she banned her staff from deploying the J-word. And I think she just might be on to something.

Anyone who knows me would never say I'm demure. And yet at times I too lean on the J-word in a bid to dilute a request. I'm not saying that softeners are never required, but these words expose the internalised limits women put on themselves because they fear they'll be disliked, and ultimately penalised, for being too straight-talking. When I was asked to do an online TEDx talk on ambition, I interviewed academics about this very phenomenon, and discovered it even has a name: the dominance penalty. The thinking goes that when women behave assertively at work, they face a choice between being successful and being liked, whereas when men display the same characteristics, they're rewarded without their popularity diminishing. Sound horribly familiar?

Whenever I find myself dwelling on the issue of female ambition, I find myself returning to a much-loved quote from the actress Roseanne Barr: 'The thing women have got to learn is that nobody gives you power. You just take it.' Only now do I realise the irony that the word 'just' has crept in – but the sentiment of her message remains true.

Activity 4

Copy and complete the analytical template on pages 133–134. Once you have done as much as you can, carry out the tasks below.

1. Consider both Text C and Text D. Copy and complete the table below (one table for each text).

2. Choose relevant quotations to analyse and copy them into the table (one quotation has been selected to start you off).

3. Use the second column to identify the ideas and attitudes that are being put forward in each quotation. Use the third column to linguistically analyse the quotation. In the exam, it won't be possible to cover all there is to say about the text – it is your job to select the most significant points about representation and to carefully analyse quotations using linguistic terms.

Quotations from Text C	Views and attitudes shown: *what* is being said about language?	Linguistic analysis: *how* are the ideas presented?
'another detrimental phrase in your lexicon keeping you from being taken seriously as a woman: "Just".'		

 Tip

Try to avoid writing out very long quotations in your exam as this wastes time. Copy out the most important parts of the quotation; you could use elliptical dots to miss out the less important parts. Just make sure that the quotation you use actually contains the point you want to make and that this is clear to the examiner. You could underline key words from the quotation to do this.

Key term

Patois: An alternative term for Creole, sometimes spelled 'patwa' to distance the language from apparent connections with Europe, and to suggest how it should be pronounced.

Paired texts 3

Read Texts E and F. Text E is taken from a longer article by Nick Harding published in *The Daily Mail* in 2013. Text F is an opinion piece by Nikesh Shukla published in *The Guardian* from 2013.

Text E

Why are so many middle-class children speaking in Jamaican patois? A father of an 11-year-old girl laments a baffling trend

By Nick Harding PUBLISHED: 11 October 2013

With her ear glued to her mobile phone, my 11-year-old daughter, Millie, was deep in conversation, her brow furrowed as she discussed some arrangement with a friend.

I listened in, as I made jam in the kitchen. 'Lol, that's well sick!' Millie said. 'DW, yolo!'

This indecipherable code-speak ('sick' means awesome, 'DW' is don't worry and 'yolo' means you only live once) was delivered in an accent I could only place as somewhere between South London, downtown Los Angeles and Kingston, Jamaica.

It certainly isn't indigenous to our home village of Ashtead, in the rolling Surrey hills.

When Millie ended the call, she turned to me, smiled and asked: 'What's for supper please, Dad?' in perfect Received Pronunciation.

It seems that after less than a month at secondary school, my daughter is now bi-lingual – but it is not French or German in which she is suddenly fluent.

Her new language, comprising alien words and abbreviations delivered with faux West Coast American inflections, will not stand her in good stead when she embarks on a school trip to visit museums in Berlin.

Millie now speaks a version of what academics call 'Multicultural Youth English', or MYE, which she has picked up from her friends – middle-class girls from the Home Counties.

Many well-heeled parents with children who have started secondary school this term will, like me, be familiar with this change in the way their children speak.

Some will be frustrated, while others will be depressed that their youngsters are conversing in what I can only describe as a clumsy rap-speak derived, variously, from the West Indies, Mumbai, MTV and American reality TV stars the Kardashians.

Initially dubbed 'Multicultural London English' by linguists, this bizarre way of speaking is now creeping out of the city and into the shires, infecting children like some linguistic superbug.

I greet my daughter's new vernacular with puzzled bemusement.

While I sometimes tire of yanking the grammatical reins and worry that this dialect will spill over from the playground into Millie's everyday life, I actually thank heavens she isn't speaking that particular version of MYE favoured by teenage boys through Middle England: the hideous dialect known as Jafaican, which seems to be spreading rapidly.

It differs from Amerifaican in that the influence is mainly Jamaican, yet it has been adopted by boys of all races and colours.

Text F

Rhyming slang is nang

Nikesh Shukla

The old East End dialect is moving out to Essex, says one academic. Come back and chill, cockneys

The East End done changed, blud. All the cockneys moved out. They decided that the only way was Essex and they dusted. They left the ends, taking their rhyming slang with them. Now the East End ain't cor-blimey-apples-and-pears-let's-ave-a-butchers – or so Queen Mary, University of London, thinks anyway.

Rhyming slang moving east of east ain't a par. It's just real life, you get me. I thought that social mobility and all that reh-teh-teh was a good thing. If anything, cockneys now span a larger area than they did before – Essex, and the home counties. If anything, it's grown.

The East End is a mirror of Britain at any given time. Now, like the rest of the country, the East End is a much more multicultural place to be. With all those different races, cotching together. And that ain't a bad thing. It's more representative of who we are as a nation.

People from Asian communities (south, south-east, the whole continent, standard), from African communities, from the Caribbean, hell, from Europe and from South America and all the trendies and hipsters with their fixies and beards, they're all here and it's hectic. We all need a new language, ya get me? A language that represents us and our manors, our yard, our ends. Cockney rhyming slang's too extra for us.

Cockney never updated. Not properly. And why should it? It never changed with the times. It's a capsule of a there and a then, a quirky and particular part of history. It's not dead though. It's shifted geographic. A migration. And they migrated a language with them. It's the same way my Gujarati family all talk in a language that hasn't been updated since they came over here in the 1960s.

All these linguist wastemen need to understand that language is also a sign of the times. Just because it's spoken in a different place to where it started, doesn't mean it's not dead. It's just moved. Think about how much of cockney comes from different languages anyway, like Yiddish ('kosher'), German ('shtoom'), Romany ('wonga'). My mum always said that loads of cockney came from Hindi. 'Pukka' is from the Hindi, meaning solid. 'Blighty' is from the Hindi bilati, meaning foreign land. 'Bandana' is from the Hindi bandhana, to tie. 'Cushti', again, from the Hindi khush, or happy. Bish-bash-bosh … No one knows where that one comes from. Except Danny Dyer.

The language of the East End now comes from grime, from hip-hop, from the internet. It comes from patois and it comes from digital Esperanto. From people like Wiley or P-Money, or whoever is currently big on road. It comes from Twitter and Facebook, from shortened words like LOL and OMFG and abbreviations like totes, and new words like humblebrag. We're absorbing content all the time, be it through free grime mixtapes or blogs and Twitter streams, and that's what's changing our language. It means something to us, who we are. That's bait.

Seeing as the East End is a multicultural place for everyone to come and cotch, don't feel like it ain't your ends anymore, cockneys. Come back. Come and chill. It's a place for everyone, innit. Just update your rhyming slang to make it more relevant. Make it more current. That ain't a bad thing. I mean, some of your rhyming slang's still used. We still say Marvin when we're hungry, or drum to mean our yard. We still drop our ts an' all.

I have some suggestions for you. Wanna do a Will this weekend (Will.I.Am = scam)? I just downloaded this criss new Leaky (leaky tap = app). Yes, blud, follow me on banana (banana fritter = Twitter). I listen to a lot of Chico mixtapes (It's Chico Time = grime). The East End will always have the bells of Bow, the 24-hour Beigel Bake in Brick Lane, the memories of fighting bare fascists on Cable Street. It'll always welcome change and be the most vibrant, diverse part of the country. That's its beauty. The cockneys dashed the East End to a next generation. And that's nang. Innit.

Activity 5

Copy and complete the analytical template on pages 133–134. Once you have done as much as you can, carry out the tasks below.

In Text E the author:

- describes and represents the kind of language his daughter is using
- links this representation to wider discourses about language
- presents an image of himself to his readers.

Using the highlighted sections below and on page 146, in the space around the text make detailed notes about how he is doing each of these things and analyse the language he is using to do them. Make sure you offer as much AO1 detail as you can in your notes.

Why are so many middle-class children speaking in Jamaican patois? A father of an 11-year-old girl laments a baffling trend

By Nick Harding PUBLISHED: 11 October 2013

With her ear glued to her mobile phone, my 11-year-old daughter, Millie, was deep in conversation, her brow furrowed as she discussed some arrangement with a friend.

> **How is he representing and positioning himself?**

I listened in, as I made jam in the kitchen. 'Lol, that's well sick!' Millie said. 'DW, yolo!'

This indecipherable code-speak ('sick' means awesome, 'DW' is don't worry and 'yolo' means you only live once) was delivered in an accent I could only place as somewhere between South London, downtown Los Angeles and Kingston, Jamaica.

> **What is significant about this word choice and what wider discourses around language might it be linked to?**

It certainly isn't indigenous to our home village of Ashtead, in the rolling Surrey hills.

When Millie ended the call, she turned to me, smiled and asked: 'What's for supper please, Dad?' in perfect Received Pronunciation.

> **How is he representing the language his daughter is using?**

It seems that after less than a month at secondary school, my daughter is now bi-lingual — but it is not French or German in which she is suddenly fluent.

Her new language, comprising alien words and abbreviations delivered with faux West Coast American inflections, will not stand her in good stead when she embarks on a school trip to visit museums in Berlin.

> **How is he representing and positioning himself?**

Millie now speaks a version of what academics call 'Multicultural Youth English', or MYE, which she has picked up from her friends — middle-class girls from the Home Counties.

How is he representing and positioning himself?

Many well-heeled parents with children who have started secondary school this term will, like me, be familiar with this change in the way their children speak.

Some will be frustrated, while others will be depressed that their youngsters are conversing in what I can only describe as a clumsy rap-speak derived, variously, from the West Indies, Mumbai, MTV and American reality TV stars the Kardashians.

How is he representing the language his daughter is using?

Initially dubbed 'Multicultural London English' by linguists, this bizarre way of speaking is now creeping out of the city and into the shires, infecting children like some linguistic superbug.

What is significant about the ways in which he describes the language here and what wider discourses around language might it be linked to?

I greet my daughter's new vernacular with puzzled bemusement.

How is he representing and positioning himself?

While I sometimes tire of yanking the grammatical reins and worry that this dialect will spill over from the playground into Millie's everyday life, I actually thank heavens she isn't speaking that particular version of MYE favoured by teenage boys through Middle England: the hideous dialect known as Jafaican, which seems to be spreading rapidly.

It differs from Amerifaican in that the influence is mainly Jamaican, yet it has been adopted by boys of all races and colours.

Key term

Illiteracy: The inability to read or write.

Stretch

Read the blog written for Manchester Metropolitan University by the linguist Rob Drummond found at: http://www.mcys-mmu.org.uk/youth-language-and-prejudice/.

He takes a very different perspective on youth language and multiethnolects. What ideas from Drummond's piece could you use to challenge and critique the arguments in Texts E and F?

Paired texts 4

Read Text G and Text H about online language. Text G is an article in the Art and Design section of *The Guardian* from May 2015. Text H is from *News Corp Australia Network* website's technology section in May 2015.

Text G

Emoji is dragging us back to the dark ages – and all we can do is smile

With its poodles, noodles and happy poos, Emoji is now the fastest growing language in the UK. What a huge step back for humanity

Jonathan Jones | Wednesday 27 May 2015 14.40 BST

So it's official. We are evolving backwards. Emoji, the visual system of communication that is incredibly popular online, is Britain's fastest-growing language according to Professor Vyv Evans, a linguist at Bangor University.

The comparison he uses is telling – but not in the way the prof, who appears enthusiastic about emojis, presumably intends. 'As a visual language emoji has already far eclipsed hieroglyphics, its ancient Egyptian precursor which took centuries to develop,' says Evans.

Perhaps that is because it is easier to go downhill than uphill. After millennia of painful improvement, from **illiteracy** to Shakespeare and beyond, humanity is rushing to throw it all away. We're heading back to ancient Egyptian times, next stop the stone age, with a big yellow smiley grin on our faces.

The Unicode Consortium has announced 38 more of the brainless little icons that are likely to be added to the standard set next year. Demand is massive: 72% of 18- to 25-year-olds find it easier to express their feelings in emoji pictures than through the written word, according to a survey for Talk Talk mobile.

As tends to happen in an age when technology is transforming culture on a daily basis, people relate such news with bland irony or apparent joy. Who wants to be the crusty old conservative who questions progress? But the simplest and most common-sense historical and anthropological evidence tells us that Emoji is not 'progress' by any definition. It is plainly a step back.

Evans compares Emoji with ancient Egyptian hieroglyphics. Well indeed. Ancient Egypt was a remarkable civilisation, but it had some drawbacks. The Egyptians created a magnificent but static culture. They invented a superb artistic style and powerful mythology – then stuck with these for millennia. Hieroglyphs enabled them to write spells but not to develop a more flexible, questioning literary culture: they left that to the Greeks.

These jumped-up Aegean loudmouths, using an abstract non-pictorial alphabet they got from the Phoenicians, obviously and spectacularly outdid the Egyptians in their range of expression. The Greek alphabet was much more productive than all those lovely Egyptian pictures. That is why there is no ancient Egyptian Iliad or Odyssey.

In other words, there are harsh limits on what you can say with pictures. The written word is infinitely more adaptable. That's why Greece rather than Egypt leapt forward and why Shakespeare was more articulate than the Aztecs.

Ancient American civilisations that used visual symbols as a language were oddly similar to Egypt in their mixture of grandeur and stasis. The Maya carved beautiful language icons, yet never developed metalwork, let alone tragic drama. There really is strong evidence that the abstract written word is essential to advance ideas, poetry and argument to their highest levels.

Speak Emoji if you want. I'll stick with the language of Shakespeare.

Text H

Linguists launch war of words on emoji as a language debate

Is emoji a language or is it just a bit of fun with a smiley face? Linguists might not agree but emoji is certainly changing how we communicate.

Rod Chester National technology writer

News Corp Australia Network MAY 21, 2015 2:42PM

Some language experts are calling emoji the fastest growing language. Others, were they to judge that view in emoji form, would be likely to use the symbol of a smiling pile of poo.

Emoji is a set of pictographs that evolved in Japan in the 1990s and are, at the very least, changing the way we communicate.

It might not qualify as a language but it is certainly a common device we turn to for electronic communication which lacks the nuances of expression and tone that help us decode verbal exchanges.

The history of emoji is traced to Japan in the late nineties, when telecommunications companies introduced the simple pictures as a way of appealing to the youth market.

Had the images been a copyrighted system, emoji might have been a fad that never took off. Instead, they are governed by the not-for-profit Unicode Consortium that sets out a code of more than 1000 emoji which people can exchange regardless of their brand of device or operating system.

Instagram this month revealed that 40 per cent of text on the photo sharing social media contains emoji. A recent British survey found that eight in ten people now use emoji in their emails and texts.

SwiftKey, the makers of third-party keyboards for smartphones, recently released a report on the global differences in emoji use, analysing more than 1 billion pieces of data sent by speakers of 16 languages in a four-month period.

The report found that Australians use alcohol and junk food emoji twice as much as the global average and holiday emoji 60 per cent more.

The study highlights that emoji use can, like words and parts of language, peak in use in line with current affairs. According to the SwiftKey study, Australians use the rabbit emoji more than anyone else in the world although it's notable that the study coincided with the South Sydney Rabbitohs winning the ARL grand final.

There are many strange cultural quirks with emoji. Americans use the princess twice as much as the English, Canadians lead the world in the use of the phallic eggplant emoji, Malaysians rule with the sleepy emoji and Arabic and Vietnamese speakers top the poll with bikinis. And one emoji symbol can have a meaning in one country that it doesn't have when used in another.

Dr Vyv Evans, a linguistics professor at Bangor University in the United Kingdom, made headlines this week with his statement that emoji was 'the fastest growing form of language ever'.

Certainly, some people have embraced emoji in a way that others would find extreme.

New York couple Liza Stark and Alex Goldmark, in an effort to test their communication skills, became a news story last year when they spent a month communicating just by emoji.

Professor Evans's labelling of emoji as 'the fastest growing language' has got many linguists talking.

Tyler Schnoebelen, a linguist who wrote his Stanford doctorate thesis on **emoticons** and emoji, dismissed the 'emoji as a language' theory in a discussion last week on the US National Public Radio show Science Friday.

'I would love to be able to say yes but you don't have children acquire this from infancy and going and developing rules,' he said.

'We don't have a way of communicating really intricate syntax things that real languages have. So it's really an important expressive resource for us but it's not a language itself.

'This is a really beautiful way to be expressive and to help refine what you tend to communicate.'

Canadian linguist Gretchen McCulloch this week tweeted a challenge to those who want to describe emoji as a language.

'New rule: anyone who wants to say that emoji are language must make that assertion entirely in emoji. Should be no problem if they're right,' she tweeted.

'They're totally fun! I like emoji! But not every way of communicating is equivalent to language.'

Dr Pauline Bryant, a Visiting Fellow at the Australian National University's linguistics program, said emoji was not a language because it did not have grammar, or an accepted structure for the order symbols should be used in communication.

'To be a language, it has to have rules to how you put the words, the symbols, together. And this doesn't,' she said.

> **Key term**
>
> **Emoticon:** A blend word, consisting of 'emotion' and 'icon', which refers to symbols that express the attitude of a writer in digital contexts where non-verbal elements are missing.

Activity 6

Copy and complete the analytical template on pages 133–134. Once you have done as much as you can, carry out the tasks below.

In the following table, some extracts from Text G have been selected for you to study more closely.

1. Complete either the AO3 or AO1 column for each extract to explore what ideas are being put forward and how language is being used by the writer to do this.

2. Once you have done this, use the final column to write a short paragraph that integrates the two elements of AO1 and AO3. An example has been offered at the start.

Extract	AO3	AO1	Integrated analytical paragraph
So it's official. We are evolving backwards.	A sense of authority and certainty is conveyed through the use of 'official' in the opening sentence and the statement of fact in the second sentence.	The writer uses two declarative statements as a headline for the whole article. The first uses the adjective 'official' and the second makes use of the present progressive.	By opening the article with a line that sounds authoritative and 'official', the article offers a very clear view. This sense of certainty is supported by the use of declarative sentences and what appears to be a simple statement of fact that technology is negatively affecting language users. The present progressive 'are evolving' helps to suggest this is happening now and is therefore a threat.
We're heading back to ancient Egyptian times, next stop the stone age, with a big yellow smiley grin on our faces.	A discourse of decline is presented here with the sense that language users are going back in time if they use emojis.		

Extract	AO3	AO1	Integrated analytical paragraph
Who wants to be the crusty old conservative who questions progress?		The **rhetorical question** is split into two clauses and the second, relative clause 'who questions progress' adds an extra level of detail to the first clause.	
These jumped-up Aegean loudmouths, using an abstract non-pictorial alphabet they got from the Phoenicians, obviously and spectacularly outdid the Egyptians in their range of expression.		A very formal and specialist vocabulary is used here with noun phrases such as 'These jumped-up Aegean loudmouths' and 'an abstract non-pictorial alphabet'.	
Speak Emoji if you want. I'll stick with the language of Shakespeare.	The writer positions himself as distinct from – and better than – emoji users.		

Key term

Rhetorical question: A question that is posed for its persuasive effect and not because the speaker really expects an answer.

Paired texts 5

Read Texts I and J. Text I is an extract from an article from *The Mail Online* published in May 2012. Text J consists of three online comments from readers in response to Text I and featured after the article.

Text I

Don't talk garbage!… or why American words are mangling our English

By Christopher Stevens for The Daily Mail

30 May 2012

The most delicate tool ever invented is the English language. It is endlessly rich, subtle, mellifluous and diverse – a vast mechanism built from 220,000 words, perfectly formed components that work together like jewelled cogs.

To wreck that mechanism deliberately – and to teach our children to do the same – would be worse than obscene. But that is what is happening.

A survey of 74,000 short stories written by British children has revealed that Americanisms are destroying traditional British words.

Like the grey squirrels that were introduced into the UK from the U.S. 130 years ago – and have almost wiped out our indigenous (and much lovelier) red squirrels – American words are infectious, destructive and virulent. And they are taking over.

American words are designed to be easy to use. They are simple to say and spell. They combine nouns and verbs, labels and instructions, so that they are convenient to pick up and apply. A country of immigrants, speaking a dissonant babel of Yiddish, Italian, Gaelic, Dutch, Norwegian, German, Polish and Russian, needed a common tongue.

Take sidewalk, for instance: it refers to that part of a road (the side) reserved for pedestrians (who walk). Two simple words are compounded to replace a third, pavement.

Yet pavement is a wonderful word, a fragment of old French that resonates with the ringing blows of medieval craftsmen as they laid a stone floor – pavire is the Latin word for beating or ramming down. Why must we in Britain discard a beautiful, meaningful word, and replace it with a Frankenstein creation?

American-English is a compound language – a language in kit form. Any word can perform any function. Listen to the jargon of a burger-flipper at a fast-food restaurant: 'Welcome to the drivethru,' 'What's your order?' 'Do you want fries with that?' 'I've actioned it,' 'Have a nice day.'

Drivethru might be the worst of all possible words. It takes a verb and a preposition, and screws them together (Americans love doing that: walkup, stopover, hangout). Then it mangles the spelling.

Finally, it applies this hideous, mongrel expression to a place where the food isn't fit for dogs.

In English, you can order your food, but food isn't an order; you can fry potatoes, but they'll be chips, not fries; you can take action and see action, but you can't simply action anything.

The findings of the survey, by the Oxford University Press, revealed yesterday that British children no longer know the difference between real English and its half-delinquent American cousin.

U.S. English is sometimes called globish, bundling 'global' and 'English' into one concept. And as we know, some Americans have a rare ability to bundle all kinds of words together.

George W. Bush was capable of saying: 'They misunderestimated me,' and 'Is our children learning?' This was a president who treated English the way a horde of squatters treat a stately home – barging in, kicking holes in the walls, and generally leaving it in a foul mess.

Of course, language is not a fixed thing that must not be tampered with. It has been evolving for 1,500 years, and in that time English has absorbed the vocabularies and grammars of half the world, as traders, invaders and refugees brought new words and ways of speaking to these shores.

It has been shaped and honed by the greatest poets who ever spoke in any tongue, from Chaucer and Shakespeare to John Betjeman and Dylan Thomas.

But the coarse, half-articulate version called American-English is not an evolution. It's a degraded version.

Two centuries ago, British abolitionists fought the American slave trade. Now a new campaign of abolition is needed – to rid us of American-English.

For everyone who is fed up of hearing drugstore instead of chemist; windshield instead of windscreen; hood instead of bonnet; cookbook instead of cookery book; gas instead of petrol; cranky instead of irritable; smart instead of clever and subway instead of underground – we do not have to tolerate it. Throw these words out!

In Minnesota and Mississippi, the inhabitants are welcome to talk as they wish. But in Birmingham, Blackburn and Barnstaple, we do not have to mimic them.

We need not replace our dustbin lorries with garbage trucks, our newspaper cuttings with clippings, our courgettes with zucchinis, our drawing pins with thumbtacks.

And we must resist all pressure to add prepositions to words that don't require them. It's fine to meet a friend – there's no need to 'meet with' anyone. Why would you want to 'reach out to' someone when you can just ask?

It [British English] contains words such as foist, for a start. And burgeoning. And mellifluous, a word I used at the top of this page: it comes from the Latin words mel, or honey, and fluere, meaning flow.

Flowing like honey – that is just what our language does. And that's the way that British children should learn to speak it.

Text J

James Marshall Rochester, Kent, UK

What a stupid article, I only hope the author wasn't paid for it. A language must evolve or its use will die out. What makes English one of the most widely used and influential languages is the fact that it has changed and adapted to influences from those who have come to use it as a **second language** and in many cases adopted it as their own. Just because it is called 'English' doesn't make it 'Ours'. The language itself was born from Germanic and Latin influence and has changed repeatedly over the years. Whether or not you agree with these changes is a moot point. Its adaptability leads to its longevity and continued use throughout the world. It has evolved and moved on, time the author of this article did as well.

Click to rate ⇧ **45** ⇩ **19**

John, Farnborough

What a stupid xenophobic article. Language evolves constantly – we may as well bemoan the fact that we no longer speak Shakespearean English. American English is no better or worse than the 'mother tongue', and in the age of globalisation and the Internet, it is inevitable that the two will intermingle.

Click to rate ⇧ **56** ⇩ **18**

Lynneguist, Brighton, UK

This is a misrepresentation of the Oxford University Press study. The study was of children's short stories. Yes, they noticed Americanisms – but the children were writing fiction that was often (the study said) inspired by novels they know – some of which are American. If you are writing a story about vampires in Oregon, then your use of 'sidewalk' doesn't indicate that you don't know the difference between American and British English. Instead, it may very well indicate that you are sensitive enough to issues of language to put the correct dialect into the mouths of your characters. I won't bother pointing out the hypocrisies and contradictions in the article. I just find it ironic that such sloppy reasoning and poor fact-checking is used to imply that Americans and their language are simple or stupid.

Click to rate ⇧ **50** ⇩ **6**

Key term

Second language (L2): The second language learned by an individual.

Stretch

Think about the views expressed in Text I and the ways in which the writer represents American and British English. Write one page (around 250–300 words) of analysis of this text in which you try to address the key points Stevens is making, the ways in which he represents his subject matter and the language techniques he is using.

Make sure you include the following:

- an introduction that explains what the subject matter is and what the author is saying about it

- discussion of at least three specific examples, supported by quotations from the text

- some consideration of the discourses being offered

- close focus on at least two different language levels.

Activity 7

Copy and complete the analytical template on pages 133–134. Once you have done as much as you can, carry out the tasks below.

Think about Text I and Text J together and start to draw out comparisons between the ways in which language is being represented. A few examples have been selected below.

	Text I	Text J
1.	Like the grey squirrels that were introduced into the UK from the U.S. 130 years ago – and have almost wiped out our indigenous (and much lovelier) red squirrels – American words are infectious, destructive and virulent. And they are taking over.	Language evolves constantly – we may as well bemoan the fact that we no longer speak Shakespearean English. American English is no better or worse than the 'mother tongue', and in the age of globalisation and the Internet, it is inevitable that the two will intermingle.
2.	The findings of the survey, by the Oxford University Press, revealed yesterday that British children no longer know the difference between real English and its half-delinquent American cousin.	This is a misrepresentation of the Oxford University Press study. The study was of children's short stories. Yes, they noticed Americanisms – but the children were writing fiction that was often (the study said) inspired by novels they know – some of which are American.
3.	Of course, language is not a fixed thing that must not be tampered with. It has been evolving for 1,500 years, and in that time English has absorbed the vocabularies and grammars of half the world, as traders, invaders and refugees brought new words and ways of speaking to these shores … But the coarse, half-articulate version called American-English is not an evolution. It's a degraded version.	The language itself was born from Germanic and Latin influence and has changed repeatedly over the years. Whether or not you agree with these changes is a moot point. Its adaptability leads to its longevity and continued use throughout the world. It has evolved and moved on…

Analyse the different ways in which the text producers of Texts I and J represent their views. On separate paper, make detailed notes on each contrasting set of views in the table above, concentrating on AO4 – the connections between the texts. Try to address the following:

- how the writers use language similarly and/or differently to express their views and address their audiences

- the views themselves and how they are part of wider discourses around language

- the contexts of production and reception and the nature of the texts themselves.

Activity 8

Now that you've worked on a range of texts on diversity and change, applied the analytical template and carried out a range of activities, choose a paired set and write up a full Question 3 response to the following exam-style question:

> Analyse how language is used in the two texts to present views about the nature of language change. In your answer you should:
>
> • examine any similarities and differences you find between the two texts
>
> • explore how effectively the texts present their views.
>
> **[40 marks]**

Activity 9

Choose one or two of the activities that you have completed in this section and apply the methods you used but to a different text. For example, you could revisit Texts C and D, and complete your own table like the one used in Activity 4. The activities in these sections are designed to be adaptable so revisit as many as you can and apply the methods used to the analysis of a different text, or pair of texts.

Dealing with AO2

Question 4 in Section B of Paper 2 asks you to produce a piece of 'opinion-based writing' that 'assesses the ideas and issues' raised in the texts you have just analysed for Question 3. Because the balance here is heavily weighted towards language knowledge (AO2), one of your main tasks is to inform the reader about how language is used and how people feel about it. Your target audience will be non-specialists so you will need to explain complex ideas and show your knowledge in a way that a new audience can understand. At the same time, you will need to address the ideas raised in Texts A and B, making sure that you understand them fully and have a clear position to take in response to them.

Organising your knowledge

One useful starting point is to go back to the texts from Question 3 and make a note of all the ideas and issues that have been raised. What are the key points to address? If you have followed the planning and note-taking guidance given in the chapter *Paper 2, Section B: Language discourses: Question 3* (pages 129–156), you will already have detailed notes on the texts provided in that section.

The next step is to think about what else you know about those ideas and issues, and how the ideas put forward in the texts relate to your understanding of the topic.

Activity 1

Thinking about the texts on MLE and youth language (Texts E and F on pages 142–144), how do the ideas about changing varieties of English and youth sociolects compare to those that you have studied elsewhere in your course? Think about the questions and ideas below and on separate paper, make a note of what you think.

1. Do young people often use language that differs from the language of their parents' generation?

2. Has language changed in London and the surrounding area in the ways that the author of Text F claims?

3. Is it fair to say that parents cannot decipher this 'code-speak'?

4. Which linguists have studied youth sociolect and what have they observed about it?

5. Have you come across the terms Multicultural Youth English (MYE) or Amerifaican before?

6. When the author of Text E describes his daughter as 'bilingual' and moving from 'MYE' to 'perfect Received Pronunciation', he is observing which linguistic process at work?

7. Which wider discourses about language can you see at work in Text E and what agenda is being pushed? What is your evaluation of this approach?

Activity 2

Read Text A below, the opening of an article in *The Daily Telegraph* about gender and conversational styles. Key ideas in the text have been highlighted and annotated with notes to link what is in this article to wider ideas from language study.

Clearly, this part of the article is making use of one area of research into gender, but there are many others that you could refer to as an A level English Language student. While the author's tone is quite ironic and suggests she thinks it isn't as simple as the Mars and Venus model, she doesn't spell this out here. Think about alternative models that you have studied and different ways of viewing language diversity. How would you challenge some of these ideas and offer alternatives? Write your ideas on a separate piece of paper.

The blend of *men* + *English* creates a new word to describe a supposed male communication style. This links to the *difference model* of gender and interaction (Tannen, Gray et al)

The idea that women and men speak entirely different languages is clearly an exaggeration, but the onus on women being the ones to adapt is one that is noted by linguists such as Deborah Cameron.

The picture and ironic caption help establish a discourse of miscommunication and relationship turmoil, again supporting the sense of difference.

The address towards women establishes them as the target audience and again the ones who need to understand male language, not vice versa.

Text A

How to speak 'Menglish'– the language 'only men' understand

Scientists have cracked it! Men and women don't understand each other because he speaks 'menglish', a report reveals. A sceptical Rebecca Holman tries to learn a new language.

He can't understand you, love, he speaks Menglish

 By Rebecca Holman
1:30PM GMT 31 Jan 2014
🐦 Follow 3,502 followers

Women's Life
Women »
Wonder Women
Columnists »
Rebecca Holman »
Men »

Trouble attracting a man? Do you find yourself inexplicably single while less attractive friends snap up men all around you? Fear not, for now we have a solution – you simply need to become more magnetic and learn *Menglish*.

Menglish, for the uninitiated, is a same-but-different language that only men speak. It looks and sounds exactly the same as normal (women's) English, but words and phrases have entirely different subtle meanings, thus leading to catastrophic (CATASTROPHIC!) communication issues between the sexes.

But don't worry, international love and relationship expert (actual job title) Julie-Anne Shapiro is an expert on menglish, has just sent me a highly illuminating press release translating what men are REALLY saying for us. Because men are from Mars and women are from Venus – AND WE'RE SPEAKING COMPLETELY DIFFERENT LANGUAGES.

> The playful description of 'normal' language being women's language ironically echoes the **deficit model** of Otto Jespersen who treated male language as the norm and women's language as a deficient version of it.

> This references John Gray's book *Men Are From Mars, Women Are From Venus* – a direct reference to the difference model.

Stretch

Read the rest of the article on the *Daily Telegraph* website and examine how Rebecca Holman's argument develops. It can be found at: http://www.telegraph.co.uk/women/womens-life/10608094/How-to-speak-Menglish-the-language-only-men-understand.html

Key term

Deficit model: An assumption that something is lacking or deficient.

Showing your knowledge

Once you have identified the key ideas and issues, and started to put together a set of wider points to bring into your answer, you will then need to organise that material into a line of argument. The question asks you to 'assess the ideas and issues raised in Text A and Text B and argue your own views', so you will need to map out an argument that you wish to make.

To achieve good AO2 marks you will need to do the following:

- go beyond the ideas in the texts themselves

- show detailed understanding of research and ideas about the topic

- give clear examples to illustrate points

- look at different ideas and start to argue a case about why these ideas are significant

- offer a clear evaluation of different views and challenge simplistic language ideas.

How could you do this for the text you have just looked at (Text A)? Here are some suggestions.

- Provide a brief historical overview of the different views about gender and interaction. You could consider an approach such as the '4D' models (deficit, dominance, difference, diversity) to help you explain this.

- Take a simple starting point – that men and women use language differently – and look at the evidence for and against this claim.

- Use the specific features being addressed in the article – a unique male style – as a starting point, but offer a challenge to such a reductive view. Do all men – or all women, for that matter – use the same style? Obviously not.

- Challenge the whole idea of gender differences in speech from the outset and build an argument that offers a broader and more diverse view of language use.

Dealing with AO5

The other aspect of an answer to Question 4 is to write a convincing, coherent piece that engages the reader and conveys your knowledge in a way that is both accessible and informative.

Writing for non-specialist readers

Part of your job in the directed writing task is to explain linguistic concepts to a non-specialist audience. This means that you need linguistic ideas to explain, and you need to develop a way of making them clear, engaging and intelligible to your readers.

In practice, this means you will need to do the following:

- Explain who researchers and theorists are and why you are quoting them or referring to them.

- Give a clear explanation of any technical terms (and show examples of them in use).

- Untangle complicated ideas and make them clear and accessible for your audience.

- Present different arguments and identify where they are coming from.

- Show an overview of issues from which you can then select relevant examples.

- Demonstrate language practices in use with examples that your readers will understand.

- Engage your readers with an effective headline and strapline.

- Show your own line of argument and guide your readers through the topic.

Opinion pieces appear in a variety of publications, both physically and online, and it is a good idea to study a range of these to get a sense of what you should be writing. It is also important to show your creativity by making the piece lively and interesting to read.

Activity 3

Go back to the pairs of texts that you analysed in the chapter *Paper 2, Section B: Language discourses: Question 3.* Select a range of texts and use the AO2 and AO5 mark schemes to evaluate how successful these texts are at engaging the reader and explaining ideas about language to their audiences. For example, in the case of Text F, is enough done to make the contemporary slang clear to an older audience? Is it appropriate for a broadsheet newspaper to refer to language researchers as 'linguist wastemen'? Are there any examples from these texts that you could adapt for your own writing, or even approaches that you really *don't* like that you think you should avoid?

An understanding of the *genre* you are writing in is vital. Text B is an annotated example of an article from *The Guardian* online by Stan Carey. Look at the highlighted areas and the corresponding comments at the sides.

Text B

Headline: playfully uses some examples of the kind of slang and dialect that is featured in the article.

Strapline/standfirst: the key message of the article is given in a more straightforward way than we see in the headline.

Key terms

Byline: A line below the headline of a newspaper article that gives the name of the writer.

Strapline: The subsidiary headline at the start of a newspaper article.

Opinion Schools

There's nowt wrong with dialects, nothing broke ass about slang
Stan Carey

Policing children's language encourages them to think nonstandard English is substandard. Linguistic diversity should be celebrated, not banned
Tue 3 May 2016 14.57 BST

f y ✉   ⤓ ▢
                                    2,276 432

▲ 'Our dialect and language use are part of our identities, connecting us to time, place, community, and self-image.' Cheryl Cole has a strong Geordie accent. Photograph: Graham Whitby Boot/Allstar

Byline: writer identifies himself, making it clear that this is a personal stance being given.

A suitable picture and caption are included to support the main themes of the article.

Tuesday 3 May 2016 – *The Guardian*

The publication is identified.

The article begins with a broad sociolinguistic point.

Language use is one of the last places where prejudice remains socially acceptable. It can even have official approval, as we see in attempts to suppress slang and dialects at school. Most recently, Ongar Academy in Essex launched a project to discourage students from using words like ain't, geezer, whatever, like, and literally.

A more specific news story is mentioned offering a 'peg' to hang the wider language discussion upon.

The specific story is now linked to a wider discourse around schools and their policing of language.

We've been here before. Schools across the country have outlawed inoffensive words, with some asking parents to 'correct' children at home. Slang, regionalisms, and colloquialisms are typical usages objected to, with occasional spelling errors thrown in as though somehow equivalent. The only thing uniting them is that they're not considered standard or sufficiently formal.

A linguist is quoted and we are told who she is.

… Linguistic vetoes can be counterproductive pedagogically too. Sociolinguist Julia Snell argues that 'to learn and develop, children must participate actively in classroom discussion; they must think out loud, answer and ask questions'. When the focus is on the forms of speech instead of its content, she writes, 'children may simply remain silent in order to avoid the shame of speaking "incorrectly", and miss the interactions crucial to learning'. In light of this I can't share Ongar Academy's satisfaction that its students are now policing each other's speech.

Snell's point is linked to Carey's own here and he draws on her argument to support his own views.

People feel strongly about correctness in language, but this strength of feeling isn't always matched by knowledge and tolerance. And because children are sensitive to how they're perceived, stigmatising their everyday speech can be harmful. By educating them about linguistic diversity instead of proscribing it, we can empower students and deter misguided pedantry.

There's nowt wrong with regional dialects, nothing broke ass about slang. They're part of our identities, connecting us to time, place, community, and self-image. They needn't be displaced by formal English — we can have both. As David Almond wrote, in a wonderful response to one school's linguistic crackdown: 'Ye hav to knaa the words the world thinks is rite and ye have to knaa how to spel them rite an speek them rite … But ye neva hav to put the otha words away.'

A link is made back to the headline, giving a sense of **cohesion** to the whole piece.

Key term

Cohesion: The way sentences or utterances join together to form a whole text.

He chooses someone else's words to conclude, making us see how effective non-standard English can be in a different context.

A grasp of style is equally important. Text C is taken from a longer article by Ann Friedman on the website of *The Cut*, a US publication. Look at the highlighted areas and the corresponding comments at the sides.

Text C

As someone who's never been shy about opening her mouth and telling you exactly what she thinks, this barrage of information about the problems inherent in women's speech has me questioning my own voice. Here I am, thinking that I'm speaking normally and sharing my thoughts on campaign-finance reform or the Greek debt crisis or the politics of marriage, when apparently the only thing that other people are hearing is a passive-aggressive, creaky mash-up of Cher Horowitz, Romy and Michele, and the Plastics. I'm as much a fan of these fictional heroines as the next woman, but I want people to hear what I'm saying and take me seriously.

At first blush, all of this speaking advice sounds like empowerment. Stop sugarcoating everything, ladies! Don't hedge your requests! Refuse to water down your opinions! But are women the ones who need to change? If I'm saying something intelligent and all a listener can hear is the way I'm saying it, whose problem is that?

The author speaks about herself in the 3rd person to begin with and then in the 1st person, representing an image of herself as forthright and unafraid of expressing her opinions.

By offering an initial take on the topic with one view – that women are being given 'empowering' advice – she can later move on to reassess this and consider alternative views.

The writer then challenges this initial view with two rhetorical questions of her own, opening up the debate for more scrutiny.

She uses a deliberately hyperbolic style to describe the negative impression she thinks she might be creating through her use of vocal fry and makes reference to popular culture that her audience might be expected to relate to or recognise.

Friedman makes use of patterned syntax (three imperative sentences punctuated with exclamation marks) to create an ironic sense of someone being given direct advice.

Relevant ideas from language study are explained here in a way that all readers can understand. There is no overly complex terminology, and different views are put forward clearly through Lakoff's words.

'All the discussion is about what we *think* we hear,' the feminist linguist Robin Lakoff tells me. Lakoff is a professor emerita at the University of California, Berkeley, and, 40 years ago, pioneered the study of language and gender. 'With men, we listen for what they're saying, their point, their assertions. Which is what all of us want others to do when we speak,' Lakoff says. 'With women, we tend to listen to how they're talking, the words they use, what they emphasize, whether they smile.'

An authority on language study is mentioned and quoted here. Lakoff is introduced clearly to a non-specialist audience (giving her credentials and relevance to this debate) and her words are quoted directly.

Making use of the source texts

As outlined earlier, your task is perhaps slightly harder than that faced by these journalists because you are being asked to 'assess the ideas and issues' raised in the texts you have just analysed for Question 3. The source texts need to work as a springboard for you into wider issues and ideas. You also need to find a way to refer to these ideas and explain to your readers how you came across them, in a way that fits with the article you are writing.

Activity 4

Look at each of the examples below and identify what you think are strengths and weaknesses in what these students have written.

1. The issue of women's language being seen as inferior to men's is one that has been discussed at length by many linguists. Lakoff, Tannen, Coates and Fishman have all done studies on it and found different things.

   Strengths: _____

   _____

   _____

   Weaknesses: _____

   _____

   _____

2. Women's language is often viewed as being deficient, or as the feminist linguist Robin Lakoff put it, women are seen as showing 'powerlessness' in their speech because girls have been brought up not to use the forceful and rough styles favoured by boys. So, women end up using what might be seen as weaker language such as hedges, tag questions and weaker expletives.

   Strengths: _____

   _____

   _____

   Weaknesses: _____

   _____

   _____

3. Two recent articles about women's language put forward very negative views about how young women talk. The *Mail Online* text says that women are suffering from a 'sexy baby vocal virus' and the *Guardian* text by Naomi Wolf says that women need to empower themselves by getting rid of the language that makes them seem weak (deficit model).

Strengths: _____

_____

_____

Weaknesses: _____

_____

_____

Writing your own piece

One of the best forms of revision is to practise writing in exam conditions.

Activity 5

Using a pair of texts from the chapter *Paper 2, Section B: Language discourses: Question 3*, write an opinion piece for a publication of your choice that assesses the ideas and issues raised in the two texts and argues your own views.

Use this checklist to help you plan your own opinion piece. Think through each of these points and ensure you have covered them in your piece.

☐ Do you have a clear line of argument?

☐ Are you responding to the ideas in the texts and showing evidence of wider knowledge and ideas from language study?

☐ Are you using a lively and engaging voice and style?

☐ Do you have a clear sense of your target audience and publication?

☐ Is your headline effective?

☐ Does your strapline offer a clear enough sense of the argument to your readers?

☐ Do you introduce who you are and your expertise/credentials with a byline?

☐ Have you written an opening line that grabs your reader's attention?

☐ Have you got a 'peg' to hang your argument on?

☐ Have you written a conclusion that links back to your opening?

☐ Have you clearly signposted your argument from idea to idea, and paragraph to paragraph?

☐ Have you used accurate and effective punctuation?

☐ Have you shown clear control of style and structure choices to show your creativity and skill?

Accent: The way that people pronounce sounds.

Accent variation: The way that pronunciations vary between different speakers, or the variations a single speaker might produce in different contexts.

Acronym: Initials that can be pronounced as words (e.g. SIM).

Adjective / Adjectival: Adjectives give more information about nouns, describing the qualities of people and things.

Adverb / Adverbial: Adverbs give more information about verbs – typically, where, when and in what manner the action of the verb takes place. Adverbial elements can be phrases, so aren't necessarily single words.

Amelioration: A process whereby a word or phrase develops more positive connotations. For example, 'nice' used to mean ignorant (from the Latin 'nescire' meaning 'to not know').

Antithesis: A person or thing that is the direct opposite.

Antonym: A word that means the opposite.

Aspect: The way in which certain grammatical markings on verb forms indicate whether an action or state is ongoing. For example, the 'ing' form in 'looking' suggests continuous action: the 'ing' ending is called a 'progressive'.

Auxiliary verb: A verbs that helps other verbs. Auxiliary verbs include 'be', 'do' and 'have'.

Behaviourism / Behaviourist: Within studies of language acquisition, a notion of learned behaviour as a set of responses to stimuli.

Blending: Using parts of existing words to form a new word.

Borrowing: Incorporating words and phrases from another language.

British Black English: A wide-ranging label, but often referring to a variety used by some speakers within the Caribbean community in the UK.

Broadening: A process by which words acquire a broader reference. For example, 'hoover' can be used as a general label for vacuum cleaners, but it was formerly the name of a particular brand.

Byline: A line below the headline of a newspaper article that gives the name of the writer.

Case study: An in-depth study of a single context that can be used to offer insights for further studies or other cases.

Child-Directed Speech (CDS): The speech that parents and caregivers use to children.

Cognitive: Thinking processes in the brain.

Cohesion: The way sentences or utterances join together to form a whole text.

Colloquial: Colloquial expressions are items of everyday language used in informal contexts.

Community of practice: A group of people who share understandings, perspectives and forms of language use as a result of meeting regularly over time.

Compounding: Adding two existing words together to create a new word.

Computer-mediated communication (CMC): Human communication that takes place via the medium of computers.

Connective: A word that joins elements together, such as 'and' and 'or'. These are also called conjunctions.

Connotation: The associations that we have for a word or phrase.

Construction: In language acquisition, constructions are ready-made chunks of language that can be used productively to express many ideas. This model is also called a usage-based approach.

Convergence: In language study, changing one's language in order to move towards that of another individual.

Corpus (plural corpora): A collection of searchable language data stored on a computer.

Covert prestige: Status gained from peer group recognition, rather than public acknowledgement.

Declarative: A clause or sentence that has a statement function.

Deficit model: An assumption that something is lacking or deficient.

Density: In studies of social networks, density refers to the number of connections that people have.

Determiner: Determiners, as the name suggests, help to determine what a noun refers to. Determiners can be wide ranging in their reference, including quantity ('some', 'many'), definiteness ('the' or 'a'), possession ('my', 'our') and demonstrativeness ('these', 'those'). Demonstratives are also called deictics, or pointing words.

Dialect: A style of language used within a particular geographical region.

Dialect levelling: The way in which dialect terms have been dropping out of use.

Discourse: A stretch of language (spoken, written or multimodal) considered in its context of use. The plural use of the term – **discourses** – refers to repeated ways of talking or writing about a topic.

Discourse community: An alternative term for a **community of practice**.

Discourse structure: The internal structure of a text.

Divergence: In language study, changing one's language in order to move away from that of another individual.

Elaborated code: An idea advanced by Bernstein (and much disputed) that middle-class speakers use context-free, complex forms of language.

Emoticon: A blend word, consisting of 'emotion' and 'icon', which refers to symbols that express the attitude of a writer in digital contexts where non-verbal elements are missing.

Endearment: An affectionate term used to address someone without using the person's name.

English as a lingua franca (ELF): The role of English as a bridging language in interactions where it is not everyone's first language.

Estuary English: A recent accent variety used in south-east England which combines RP with some aspects of regional southern accents. 'Estuary' refers to the Thames Estuary area.

Ethnic identity / ethnicity: Feeling connected with people who have similar cultural backgrounds, heritage, or family ties.

Euphemistic / Euphemism: An indirect form of language that enables speakers to avoid mentioning something unpleasant or offensive.

First language (L1): The first language learned by an individual, usually in childhood.

Formal / Formality: Designed for use on serious or public occasions where people pay attention to behaviour and appearance.

Gender: The social expectations that arise as a result of being one sex or another.

Generic: For general use or general reference.

Genre: In language study, a type of text in any mode which is defined by its purpose, its features, or both. In literary fields, genre tends to refer primarily to the literary genres of prose, poetry and drama, but it can also refer to types of content (for example, crime or romance).

Grammar: The structural aspects of language that tie items together. Grammar includes syntax, or word order; and morphology, or the elements added to words to show their grammatical role (such as '-ed' to indicate the past tense of a verb).

Graphology: All the visual aspects of textual design, including colour, typeface, layout, images and logos.

Hedge: Cautious language used to make what we say less direct or certain.

Holophrastic: Holophrase means 'whole phrase' and, as it suggests, refers to the stage of language acquisition where whole phrases can be expressed via a single word. Also called the one-word stage.

Idiom / Idiomatic: An expression whose meaning is not dependent on the meanings of the words it contains. For example, saying that someone 'has a chip on their shoulder' or that something costs 'an arm and a leg'.

Illiteracy: The inability to read or write.

Inference: Using assumed knowledge in order to determine meaning.

Inferential framework: Knowledge built up over time and used in order to understand meanings that are implicit.

Inflection: A morpheme on the end of a word to indicate a grammatical relationship or category. For example, many nouns in English add an 's' to indicate plurality.

Initialism: Initials that cannot be pronounced as words (e.g. DVD).

Innate: Something inbuilt, already in place.

International English: The idea of English as a language that is used in international contexts of all kinds.

Interrogative clause: A question.

Intonation: Tunes, created from variations in pitch, that convey meaning in the speech of a particular language.

Language acquisition: The development of language within an individual.

Language reform: A term used, usually by liberal commentators, to support the idea of consciously changing language because it is considered unfair to different groups.

Lexical priming: The way in which some words appear to be ready-made for certain meanings, as a result of their habitual use in the same contexts.

Lexis: The vocabulary of a language.

Literacy: Refers primarily to reading and writing, including the new types of reading and writing that occur in digital contexts.

Matched guise technique: An experimental technique where a single actor puts on a different accent for different audiences, but keeps the content of the speech the same.

Matronyms: Names that reflect female lines of inheritance.

Meanings: Messages that are communicated. Meanings are never fixed, but are negotiated between speakers (or writers) and listeners (or readers), and vary considerably according to context.

Metaphor: A language strategy for bringing two unrelated ideas together in order to suggest a new way of looking at something. Metaphors are common where something is difficult to understand because it is complex or abstract, so it is compared with something simpler or more concrete.

Methodology: The study of different ways to research ideas.

Mode: Speech and writing are called different modes. Digital communication can draw on both of these modes, so is often called a hybrid form of communication.

Morphology: The aspect of grammar that refers to grammatical markings. For example, the 's' ending on nouns can indicate a plural form (one book, two books).

Multicultural London English: A recent variety combining elements of the language of different ethnic groups, particularly Afro-Caribbean English. The variety arose in London but has spread to different parts of the UK.

Multicultural Urban British English: A label that refers to the way in which Multicultural London English has spread to other large conurbations in the UK.

Multimodal: A multimodal text employs more than one mode of communication – for example, by using images as well as words, or by drawing on an aspect of speech as well as writing.

Multiplexity: In studies of social networks, multiplexity refers to the number of ways in which two individuals might relate to each other, for example, as friends, workmates and family members.

Narrowing: A process by which words acquire a narrower reference. For example, 'deer' used to refer to animals in general, not to a specific animal.

Nativist / Nativism: A belief that language acquisition relies on an inbuilt capacity for language in humans.

Non-regional: An alternative name for the RP accent.

Non-standard: Different from normal or majority usage.

Noun phrase: A phrase that has a noun or pronoun as its main word (called the head word).

Object: The thing or person on the receiving end of the action of the verb.

One-word stage: Also called the holophrastic stage, this refers to the stage of language acquisition where a single word can stand for a whole expression.

Orthography: The spelling system.

Overgeneralisation: Applying a rule and assuming that every example follows the same system, without realising that there are exceptions.

Overt prestige: Status that is publicly acknowledged.

Patois: An alternative term for Creole, sometimes spelled 'patwa' to distance the language from apparent connections with Europe, and to suggest how it should be pronounced.

Patronyms: Names that reflect male lines of inheritance.

Pejoration: A process whereby a word or phrase develops more negative connotations. For example, 'cunning' used to mean knowledgeable.

Phatic: Language that is devoid of content but that supports social relationships.

Phonemic alphabet: An alphabet for transcribing general sounds, suitable for a specific language. An individual sound is called a 'phoneme'.

Phonetics / Phonology: The study of the sound system. Phonetics refers to the physical production and reception of sound, while phonology is a more abstract idea about all the sounds of a particular language.

Pivot schema: The use by children of certain key words as a 'pivot' to generate many utterances.

Politeness: An aspect of pragmatics that refers to the cultural rules of a community and regulates how social relationships are negotiated. Everyday use of the term 'polite' tends to be associated with surface aspects such as table manners and saying 'please' and 'thank you'. These aspects are connected with the academic concept but it goes much deeper than this, including all aspects of cultural rules about appropriate language use in social engagements.

Political correctness: A term used, usually by conservative commentators, to object to the idea of consciously changing language because it is considered unfair to different groups.

Post-telegraphic: A developmental stage that goes beyond children's use of abbreviated speech.

Pragmatics: The study of how words are used in a particular context to create a certain meaning.

Preposition: A word that typically indicates direction, position, or relationship, such as 'into', 'on', or 'of'.

Pronoun: Pronouns can stand in place of nouns, hence the term 'pro-noun'. Standard English personal pronouns are: I, you, he, she, it, and one (singular); we, you and they (plural).

Prosodics / Prosody: Prosody is the melody that our voices create via prosodic aspects such as rhythm and intonation.

Received Pronunciation (RP): An accent traditionally associated with high social status. 'Received' refers to the idea of social acceptance in official circles.

Register: A form of specialist language. For example, the language of sport or science.

Relativiser: Another word for a relative pronoun, for example, 'which', 'who', 'that', often used at the front of a subordinate clause.

Repertoire: The range of language forms or styles used by a speaker.

Representation: Something that stands in place of something else. Representation is how something *appears* to be, not how it really *is*.

Restricted code: An idea advanced by Bernstein (and much disputed) that working-class speakers use context-based, limited forms of language.

Rhetoric / Rhetorical: Rhetoric is the study of persuasive language, an area of study dating back to ancient Greece.

Rhetorical question: A question that is posed for its persuasive effect and not because the speaker really expects an answer.

Salient: Most important.

Sapir-Whorf hypothesis: The idea, derived from the work of Edward Sapir and Benjamin Lee Whorf, that our language constructs our view of the world and that it is difficult or even impossible to think beyond it.

Scope: How far a study extends, how much is covered.

Second language (L2): The second language learned by an individual.

Semantic field: A group of terms from the same domain. For example, names for food or aspects of computer communication.

Semantic pattern: A cluster of words with similar uses.

Semantics: The meanings of words and expressions. Semantics can also refer to meaning in a broader sense, i.e. the overall meaning of something.

Slang: Language that is used in informal contexts and widely recognised (unlike dialect usage, which occurs only in particular regions).

Social group: Individuals who share interests and connections with others, or who are classified as having something in common.

Social network: A network of relations between people in their membership of different groups.

Sociolect: The dialect spoken by people of a particular social class.

Solidarity: A feeling of connection with others, mutual support.

Standard English: A language system that acts as an agreed common language, especially for formal uses. This primarily refers to the writing system of English.

Stereotype: The idea that whole groups of people conform to the same, limited, range of characteristics.

Storyboard: A set of images to represent the action within a moving text such as a TV programme or advertisement.

Strapline: The subsidiary headline at the start of a newspaper article.

Style: In language study, a distinctive way of speaking or writing for different contexts (akin to styles of dress in studies of fashion).

Subject: The thing or person carrying out the action of a verb.

Subject position: The perspective taken on a topic, where some aspects are foregrounded and emphasised while others are downplayed.

Suffix: A particle added to the end of a word.

Syntax: How words are arranged, or the word order that is typical of a language.

Tense: The way in which verbs can indicate time, for example the '-ed' ending on a verb such as 'look' indicates past time.

Transcript: A record of what speakers said and did.

Virtuous error: A mistake that has an underlying logic, showing that learning has taken place.

Vocal fry: A vocal effect where the speaker produces a rasping, creaky sound by blowing air through the vocal cords.

World Englishes: Varieties of English that are used in different countries around the world, mainly in areas that were formerly colonised, such as India and Singapore. These countries have their own version of Standard English.